♡ _Cortney, Jesse,+
Baby Colton

TO

FROM

DATE

Becoming a parent is like lacing up a pair of hiking boots and heading out on a trail you've heard all kinds of stories about but never set foot on. It's exciting! It's scary! It's fun, and messy and hard and wonderful all at once! From your first steps, you are exploring the beauty of a new little life. On some level you know that there will be ups and downs, unknowns and certainties, twisted ankles and hand-holding, boo-boos and belly laughs. But until you really embark on the parenthood adventure, you haven't yet experienced the incredible blessing that it is.

This book is designed for you, new adventurer. Each devotion offers strength for the journey and a promise from God that His love for you—and your baby—is just what you need to thrive. And step by step, as you and your baby go through life together, you'll discover that God designed your family in the most wonderful way. May the truth in these pages encourage your heart in all the ways you need it most.

OH

BABY

DEVOTIONS FOR

NEW PARENTS

DaySpring

LIVE YOUR FAITH

Oh Baby! Devotions for New Parents
Copyright © 2021 DaySpring Cards, Inc. All rights reserved.
First Edition, May 2021

Published by:

21154 Highway 16 East
Siloam Springs, AR 72761
dayspring.com

All rights reserved. *Oh Baby! Devotions for New Parents* is under copyright
protection. No part of this book may be used or reproduced in any manner
whatsoever without written permission except in the case of brief quotations
embodied in critical articles and reviews.

Scripture quotations marked CEV are from the Contemporary English Version
Copyright © 1991, 1992, 1995 by American Bible Society, Used by Permission.

Scripture quotations marked NIV are taken from THE HOLY BIBLE, NEW
INTERNATIONAL VERSION®, NIV® Copyright © 1973, 1978, 1984, 2011 by Biblica,
Inc.® Used by permission. All rights reserved worldwide.

Scripture quotations marked NKJV are taken from the New King James Version.
Copyright © 1982 by Thomas Nelson, Inc.

Scripture quotations marked NLT are taken from the Holy Bible, New Living
Translation, copyright © 1996, 2004, 2007, 2013, 2015 by Tyndale House
Foundation. Used by permission of Tyndale House Publishers, Inc., Carol Stream,
Illinois 60188. All rights reserved.

Scripture quotations marked CSB®, are taken from the Christian Standard Bible®,
Copyright © 2017 by Holman Bible Publishers. Used by permission. Christian
Standard Bible®, and CSB® are federally registered trademarks of Holman Bible
Publishers.

Scripture quotations marked NASB are taken from the NEW AMERICAN
STANDARD BIBLE ®, © Copyright 1960, 1962, 1963, 1968, 1971, 1972, 1973, 1975,
1977, 1995 by the Lockman Foundation. Used by permission. (www.lockman.org).

Scripture quotations marked NRSV are taken from the New Revised Standard
Version of the Bible, © 1989. Division of Christian Education, National Council of
Churches. Used by permission of Zondervan Publishing House, Licensee.

Scripture quotations marked TLB are taken from The Living Bible copyright
© 1971 by Tyndale House Foundation. Used by permission of Tyndale House
Publishers Inc., Carol Stream, Illinois 60188. All rights reserved. The Living Bible,
TLB, and The Living Bible logo are registered trademarks of Tyndale House
Publishers.

Scripture quotations marked NCV are taken from the New Century Version®.
Copyright © 2005 by Thomas Nelson, Inc. Used by permission. All rights reserved.

Written by Trieste Vaillancourt
Cover Design by Jessica Wei

Printed in China
Prime: J4968
ISBN: 978-1-64454-987-2

CONTENTS

YOU'VE GOT THIS

*Children are a blessing
and a gift from the LORD.*
PSALM 127:3 CEV

Long before the creation of the world, God chose your child to be conceived at this time in history—to the parents that He picked, purposed, and prepared for the job.

While the discovery of pregnancy is sometimes a tear-jerking, wonderful experience for parents—and sometimes painful and sometimes awe-inspiring—God is never, *ever* surprised. He knew it all along.

Whether a child has been longed for many years or comes as a sweet surprise, a child is most certainly a gift. Psalm 127 celebrates the ways that God blesses a home with protection, provision—and kids! Children are intended to strengthen, bless, and fill a family with love. And if we believe that God's intentions are for the absolutely wonderful, then we can be confident that He will give us everything we need to *thrive*—not just *survive*—as a family.

Hang onto the promise that God not only made your baby happen, but He did it on purpose—whether He has honored your prayers or given you a gift you weren't even asking for. He is providing for your new little one with His very best resources. And remember, nerves are normal! Unknowns are expected! Excitement is inevitable, especially as you cradle your tiny person in your arms, knowing your baby will need you to love with a kind and amount of love you may not even think you have quite yet. God is waiting to give you all you need, every day, every step of the way. And no matter what, you can be sure that He's even more excited than you are to watch the beautiful story of your family unfold.

PRAYER

Father, thank You for Your faith in us as
parents and Your faith in our family.
You know even better than we do what we
are capable of, and we will cling to You as
we seek to train up this child in Your ways.
Shepherd us as parents even as we shepherd
this child along the journey to discover
You as Lord and Savior.

YOU HAVE EVERYTHING YOU NEED

And my God will meet all your needs
according to the riches
of His glory in Christ Jesus.
PHILIPPIANS 4:19 NIV

So much preparation happens for a new baby. Rooms are painted; cribs are assembled; toys and tiny clothes and feeding supplies are stocked into shelves. Homes may be deep cleaned. Lifestyles are examined and decorations hung tenderly over changing tables and rocking chairs. Potential names are tried out to see if they make nice monograms.

Being prepared can bring some relief for parents-to-be. But the truth is, parents can only do so much to become ready for a new little one. So much of the first months (and years!) is about troubleshooting and growing through the process. Loving is an art form that comes by practice. And our very best plan of action is to turn to God, the Author of our lives and the very essence of love.

God is the Giver of every good gift, and He is very generous in His giving. There will never be a time, He says, when you'll not have exactly what you need. Sometimes that won't feel true—but in those moments, we can dig a little deeper. Wait a little longer. Look a little harder. Trust a little more. His resources are always delivered right on time (though not always early enough for us to get too confident—because relying on Him is a gift in itself too).

In the dark of night, when the baby is crying and you'd rather be sleeping, God is awake. When diapers and spills and boundary-testing toddlers bring tears to your eyes, God is aware. When friendships or bones get broken, God is a healer. When the unthinkable things—or the most wonderful things you can think of—fill your days, God is an unshakable presence every step of the way. As we learn to tap into all that He is and all that He has for us, we become the confident parents He's designed us to be.

 PRAYER

Lord, I believe You meet every need:
open my eyes to all the ways You deliver.
I believe You have my very best at heart:
help me see Your tenderness and mercy at
work. I believe You love me: sensitize me
to the feel of Your arms around me and
the sound of Your voice in my spiritual ears.
Thank You for the gift of You.

YOUR PRAYERS MAKE A DIFFERENCE

Before I formed you in the womb I knew you,
before you were born I set you apart.
JEREMIAH 1:5 NIV

The idea of being fully responsible for a tiny human can be overwhelming, especially if you haven't been in that position before! It's hard to know where to begin. But one of the most powerful things a parent can do for their child is simply to pray for them. Every day, even long before you meet your little one, your prayers are acknowledged before God.

No one in the world sees your kids like you do. No one can pray with the same insights or observations. And a parent's prayer certainly blesses God's heart. After all, He invites us as parents to communicate the same selfless love that He has for us. And because He knows we're ill-equipped to do that apart from Him, He makes Himself highly available for that very purpose. As we seek Him in parenting, He pours out His most fatherly love over us and our family. He puts people in our lives who can love, mentor, encourage, and build us on the adventure. He helps us with creative problem-solving, late nights, and more grace than we can measure.

Prayer is effective because He not only listens to us, but He also responds and tells us *great and unsearchable things* (Jeremiah 33:3 NIV). As the Artist and Creator of your little one, He put every single cell together in a very intentional way. Your baby's genetic makeup, likes and dislikes, quirks and strengths, passions and purpose are recorded in His notes. He can give you one-of-a-kind direction on how to shepherd your child through all the stages of adolescence. He chose your child for such a time as this. (He chose *you* for such a time too.) So there's no better place to turn as you embark on the adventure of loving this little one to, and through, life.

And as your life points to God, through prayer and the fruit of your relationship with Him, you'll be the very best arrow for your child to find Him too.

 PRAYER

Knowing how intentional You are
about Your children is so comforting, God.
And I know You can teach me to be intentional
in prayer with You for this family.
As I seek You, I know I'll find You.
And that partnership is priceless.

YOU CAN PARENT WITH PEACE

Seek first His kingdom and His righteousness,
and all these things will be given to you as
well. Therefore do not worry about tomorrow.
MATTHEW 6:33–34 NIV

As parents, we know that children offer constant reasons to worry. The problem comes when we realize that, first, we could try with all our ability to protect and love our children and still fall short in areas we hadn't even thought of. Second, children always seem to be inventing new ways to give parents gray hair! And third, the world we live in is cause for concern in itself.

Apart from Jesus, there's no peace. Not the real kingdom peace that Jesus promised us in John 14:27 where Jesus says, "Peace I leave with you; my peace I give you. I do not give to you as the world gives. Do not let your hearts be troubled and do not be afraid" (NIV). The great news is that His peace—the lasting, deep, real kind—is ours for the taking. In any situation, at any time, and in abundant amounts.

One thing we can be sure of, as we read and rely on Scripture, is that if God commands it, He makes it possible for us. When He commands us to seek His kingdom above the world's "treasures," that means there's a kingdom of heaven available for us to discover. If He commands us not to worry, then He gives us the ability (as we lean on Him) to *not worry*. Sounds and feels impossible at times, doesn't it?

Fortunately, God provides tools to help us in our battle of the mind. Isaiah 26:3 tells us that as we keep focused on God, He keeps us in peace. Second Corinthians 10:5 gives us the action step of taking our negative, worrisome thoughts captive—not allowing them to sabotage our peace. John 15:1–11 gives us the simple yet very challenging task of abiding in Him in order to obtain the fruit of peace.

Wondering where to start *not worrying*? Try presenting your requests to God by prayer, with thanksgiving (Philippians 4:6 NIV). Thank Him for your beautiful children, loving spouse, warm home, diaper wipes, or worship music. Think of the hot shower you can have, even if it's short because the little one is hungry. As you focus your attention on the good of His kingdom, He will lift your eyes above the mess and help you observe the world from *His* perspective—a very peaceful one indeed.

PRAYER

Jesus, thank You for Your perplexing, powerful peace. I receive it today, in Your name.

YOU ARE NOT ALONE

Whoever dwells in the shelter of the Most High
will rest in the shadow of the Almighty.
*I will say of the L*ORD*, "He is my refuge and my*
fortress, my God, in whom I trust."
PSALM 91:1–2 NIV

It can start in the first weeks of pregnancy. It grows in the delivery room and repeats multiple times throughout a child's life: an internal cry that says, "I can't do this!" Have you been there? More than likely, your heart will echo this more than once during your parenting journey.

It doesn't always matter whether you have a supportive spouse or family nearby. Sometimes you can be well-connected and still feel alone. Other times, your aloneness stems from being a single parent or the one who is home with the kids most of the day or night. The transition is normal. You may have been someone who thrived on long hikes through nature. You may have relied heavily on a dynamic network of social activities. But all of that changes when a baby comes! It's inevitable! Your preferences and personality don't change, but your outlets for those things suddenly become much less available.

While it's true that our lifestyle takes a sharp right turn when a baby comes, the best news is that God does *not* change. He is the one constant through it all, supporting you and loving you exactly the same on *this* side of parenthood as He did on *that* side. It may take longer than you'd like to discover your new dynamic with Him. But if you continue to trust and take it one day at a time, you will find that His hand never lets go of yours.

Psalm 91 is a resource for any struggling new parent. David experienced the highest of highs (think of killing a giant and saving a nation) and the lowest of lows (as a murderer and conspirator whose firstborn son died in infancy). He learned through his life to cry out to God in need and to proclaim the truth of who God really is. Psalm 91 declares those truths and promises. When you feel alone and overwhelmed, consider turning to Psalm 91 and remembering what is true.

PRAYER

God, I dwell in Your shelter and
find my rest in You. You alone are
my refuge and place of safety.
You are my God, and I trust You.

YOU HAVE GOD'S GRACE

Because of His great love for us ... God raised us up with Christ and seated us with Him in the heavenly realms.
EPHESIANS 2:4, 6 NIV

Being a new parent is like nothing you've ever experienced. Nothing—not babysitting, not nieces and nephews, not volunteering in the church nursery or taking classes—can prepare parents for the realities of being 100 percent responsible for a tiny human 100 percent of the time. There are amazing, beautiful highs with the experience. And there are sleep-deprived, worried, hangry, hormonal lows. In the end, the good *will* outweigh the hard. But that truth can be difficult to cling to when you're in the middle of the mess.

Ephesians 2:5–7 NIV offers a one-of-a-kind promise for those who trust in Jesus: "It is by grace you have been saved. *And God raised us up with Christ and seated us with Him in the heavenly realms in Christ Jesus,* in order that ... He might show the incomparable riches of His grace..." (emphasis added).

This promise means that Jesus leads us to a place far above our current circumstances. We might be experiencing all the challenges of new parenting—but at the same time, we can lean on God to lift us up and show us the bigger picture. By faith, we have all the grace we need to get through any challenge. With His help, an explosive diaper can be a bonding experience for you and the baby. A sleepless night can still offer refreshment through prayer over your sweet one. The next new thing to worry about can become a chance to release it to God and watch Him lead you through.

It can be *so hard* to remember this good news when you're suffering. You can do some things in your more lucid moments to help yourself out when it's tough. Note cards posted next to your favorite feeding chair can draw your eyes upward. Sticky notes on your mirror, asking your spouse to memorize Ephesians 2:5–7 with you, and regularly thanking God for your baby are all great strategies. And of course, when you're struggling, simply asking Him to show you the heavenly perspective can change your outlook in just a moment.

 PRAYER

God, thank You for being on my side.
Thank You for giving me grace.
With You at my side, I know
I'll make it through.

YOU HAVE A GOOD LEGACY

You shall expand to the right and to the left,
and your descendants will inherit the nations.
ISAIAH 54:3 NKJV

Kids are, by design, legacy *bearers*. Everything from genetics to geographical accent can be passed from one generation to another. Depending on your family situation, the knowledge that you can pass on things to your kids is either exciting or terrifying. Fortunately, God is the legacy *maker*. A parenting partnership with God will strengthen your good legacies and redeem the bad.

Sakura grew up with an alcoholic father. The history of abuse, pain, and confusion from her own childhood was enough to make her worry about raising healthy children. Could she impart pure love to her daughter when her own childhood was full of trauma? And would she, when things got tough, use alcohol to solve her problems? She was advised by a pastor friend to pour out her concerns to God and then leave them at His feet. As her daughter grew, never once did Sakura repeat the example her father set for her as a child. Instead, when times were hard, she prayed and she carried God's peace. The best part is, Sakura doesn't worry that her daughter will carry on a legacy of destruction. The cycle is broken.

Derek's grandfather started a heating and cooling company in the 1920s. Derek would toddle around the storefront as a boy while his dad and grandpa worked in the machine shop and his mom helped customers. He loved growing up in a family that worked together, but when he went to college he decided to take a different path from the family business. His degree in psychology and a satisfying marketing career have little to do with the shop his great-grandfather started. But from his family, Derek had learned important values: hard work, together time, adapting to change, and showing excellence and kindness toward people. Derek defines his career and family life as successful.

Whatever your legacy, the Lord will lead you in healing from your past and passing on the good. When you lean, He leads. That's a promise.

 PRAYER

Father, thank You for making me part of a legacy worth passing on. And today I trust You with the parts I would rather not share with my children. Make us a family that glorifies You—through our healing, our growth, and our love for You.

YOU ARE EQUIPPED TO PROTECT

*We put our hope in the LORD.
He is our help and our shield.*
PSALM 33:20 NLT

Parenting is a delicate balance between protecting our kids and letting them take risks to learn and grow. But one thing we never compromise on, as much as it depends on us, is their safety. Some children are naturally cautious. Others are of the "leap first, look second" variety. Regardless, parents often have a bird's-eye view of the situation children are in and can guide them safely through their surroundings.

Whether they realize it or not, our babies trust us. A baby doesn't worry about being fed, changed, or snuggled. She doesn't consider whether it's a good idea to suck on the dog's squeaky toy or whether it's safe to climb the nearest chair and reach for an object high on a shelf. A baby trusts his or her parent to be there no matter what. And often they don't even see the danger they could be in. Babies get upset when something is taken away from them. They are so caught up in the moment—discovering and exploring—that it often takes the more experienced eye to guide their decision-making processes. In fact, it's their childlike faith in us, their parents and protectors, that allows them to live freely and discover the world around them.

As adults, we are invited into a childlike faith. Our heavenly Father takes on the role of our Protector and Shepherd. He sees our surroundings and knows what is best for us. And as parents, we can rely on Him to keep us secure in Him as we focus on guiding our little ones.

Just as babies turn to their parent when they recognize the need, we can turn to God as often as we need. He is our shield, our help, and our most trustworthy Father. And He wants nothing more than to love us with His everlasting love.

PRAYER

Lord, it's so easy to get bogged down in "what-ifs"—to feel like I'm not adequate enough to keep my baby safe. But when I remember that You are my shield and my defender, it's easier to rest in You. I know You care more about my baby than I'll ever understand. So even as I work to keep my baby safe and well today, I trust You to cover us completely.

YOU ARE THE BEST PARENT FOR YOUR CHILD

For we are God's handiwork,
created in Christ Jesus to do good works,
which God prepared in advance for us to do.
EPHESIANS 2:10 NIV

Social media is quick to tell us that we just don't compare to other parents. By the look of people's kids and puppies, everyone else's lives are nearly perfect. As we scroll along, enviously noting their sunny vacations, intimate together times, masterfully plated meals, constantly clean clothes, and well-behaved siblings, we glance up at the dish-covered sink and crumb-covered counter. We notice that the baby left a vomit stain on one shoulder and we forgot to change our shirt before the video call we had for work.

The truth is, people rarely memorialize their less-than-perfect times on their social pages. And in much the same way, the world rarely sees the insecurities and worries we face every time we lay our head on the pillow at night. We judge others by their neatly trimmed outer lives, and we judge ourselves by our messy, disorganized, emotional insides. That, friend, is not apples to apples.

But the greater truth? You. Are. Enough. There is no better parent for your child than you. No one's education would enable them to raise your child with more beneficial expertise. No one's hug would feel better to your child than yours. No one's broccoli cuts or buttered noodles would taste better to your child—not really. Because you were created for *this* family, for *this* time, with *this* child.

Sure, everyone can learn and grow. There may be books worth reading and experts worth following. There are friends or family members worth observing in their strengths as parents. But what your child needs most is the vessel through which all of that love was made to be channeled—*you.*

Don't let anyone ever tell you that parenting isn't a ministry or a purpose. You were designed to pour into your kids for God's glory. He prepared you for this family, and He prepared this family for you. Your child will thrive as you share yourself—your whole, imperfect, beautiful self.

PRAYER

God, I believe You have made me just the right parent for my child. I acknowledge that I have many shortcomings and that I need You every day in order to do this. But in my weakness, You are strong. And I'm willing to do this together with You!

Oh, taste and see that the LORD is good.
PSALM 34:8 NKJV

Two-year-old Jenna happened to be in the right place at the right time. It was Saturday morning, and Mama had just gone to get a special and unusual treat for herself and Daddy—donuts. As Daddy bit into a round pastry with white frosting and chocolate stripes, Jenna asked, "What dat, Daddy?" Her dad tore off a small bite and stuck it into her open mouth. "That's a donut, baby. What do you think?" Jenna's eyes sparkled as her tongue touched the sugary sweetness.

"Do you like it?" Mama asked. "Uh-huh!" Jenna said with enthusiasm.

A few mornings later, Mama walked toward the door while Daddy was feeding Jenna at the kitchen table. Jenna looked up with a hopeful smile and asked, "Mama go get donuts?" She hadn't forgotten the taste of the special treat from days before. And she anticipated the goodness again.

God is full of the goodness of donuts, only infinitely more (and with much healthier benefits!). When we have the chance to experience Him in our lives, it's the taste we remember and want for the rest of our lives.

We may not recognize what we need. We may not know where to find it, especially on challenging days. But the goodness of God is what fills us, prepares us, and makes us able to thrive.

Parenthood is overflowing with opportunities to taste the goodness of God. Sometimes those moments are obvious—like first steps, first words, tender snuggles, and joyful laughter. Other moments are more an acquired taste. It can be hard to recognize through fevers or fights. But there is always something worth savoring. How? Through thankfulness. Even the reality of having children is a gift worth thanking Him for. We can thank Him for health, for enough food, for cute curly heads and tiny button toes. It is different for everyone. But every time we acknowledge those little morsel moments of goodness in our children and our days, it gets easier and easier to see how rich our lives as parents are.

 PRAYER

Father, thank You for giving so much of
Yourself through our children. Forgive me
for not recognizing the buffet of blessings I get
to enjoy every day. Help me grow in gratitude,
and refine my taste for all things You.

YOU MAKE YOUR CHILD BETTER

Parents are the pride of their children.
PROVERBS 17:6 NIV

You are the right parent for your child. All of your gifts, personality traits, quirks, strengths, and weaknesses line up with who your child needs you to be. That doesn't mean there isn't a ton of room for every parent to grow. But it does mean that there's nothing innately wrong with you that will scar your child for life!

When children are young, they think the world of their parents. They don't know any better—they even think dad jokes are funny. They willingly accept their mother's hugs and kisses. Children learn how to play, dream, process, and interact in their home setting. It's not until years later, when they become more self-aware and understand that there are as many different ways to live as there are people on the planet, that it becomes natural to question what they know. At that point, parents may become "uncool" as the young person finds their way in the world.

Jesus didn't change Himself in order to please others. He was, arguably, the most controversial person in history. He stuck to His guns as His Father's Son, loving the unlovable and teaching the truth. Imagine what would have happened if He had listened to the naysayers! What if He had backed down when it got hard, running away and refusing to submit to the process of dying on the cross so that we could live? That would have been the end of humanity. But instead, Jesus accepted His identity, rejoices when people choose Him, and intercedes on behalf of those who haven't.

You will most definitely waver between being the best and the worst parent ever throughout your child's life. But truth be told, you—just by being you—make your child a better person. As you follow the Lord in parenting, you are adding to the wonderful testimony and legacy of your children.

 PRAYER

Father, make me the kind of parent who brings joy to my children. Help me to stay consistent and strong like Jesus, even when we struggle as a family. I know that in the end, we are meant to be together for Your glory.

YOU CAN BE HAPPY

How happy is anyone
who has put his trust in the LORD.
PSALM 40:4 CSB

The Hebrew word *esher* can be translated as either "happy" or "blessed." It carries the connotation of both of those English words. People don't always see those two words as synonyms: it's possible to know that God has blessed you without feeling happy; likewise, sometimes happiness feels fleeting or different from what we normally associate with being blessed by God.

Here's a theory: What if happiness is actually a *gift* from God and not just an emotion based on our circumstances? What if we can receive happiness as readily as we can lift an Amazon package off the porch, open it up, and enjoy the fruits of one-day shipping? What if happiness is actually *very much* like receiving a blessing from God?

And what if—remember, this is a theory— true, godly happiness is the kind of gift that reveals itself only as the recipient invests? Imagine a vending machine that accepts coins. You've got a pocket full of nickels and you want a soda, which costs two dollars. You begin inserting nickels into the slot. It takes awhile, but you keep investing until you hear the mechanism inside releasing a soda into the chute. You trust that the soda will come, because that's what a vending machine is designed to do.

What if God's promise of happiness works in a similar way? We make small deposits of trust in Him every day, even moment by moment. And we begin to enjoy happiness as a way of life. The more we trust—the more we thank Him, pray, and worship Him—the happier we become. Our investments of trust, in a sense, allow Him to give us more and more satisfaction in Him and His ways.

Few things test our ability to trust in God like having a child. But as it is with so many of His principles, the greater the need, the greater the reward. Happiness that comes from surrendering our abilities and our babies, day after day, is a deep and lasting happiness that feels very much like a blessing indeed.

PRAYER

God, thank You for receiving my "nickel-sized" investments of trust every day, turning them into blessings. Give me Your perspective on happiness so that I can recognize it in my life and in the lives of my family.

YOU ARE BRAVE

Be strong and courageous.
Do not be afraid or terrified because of them,
for the LORD your God goes with you;
He will never leave you nor forsake you.

DEUTERONOMY 31:6 NIV

The book of Acts tells of Lydia, a successful business owner in the male-dominated Roman Empire. A dealer of purple cloth in Thyatira, Lydia was not unique in her trade but certainly a pioneer in her personal life. And although little is known about her family and household, we do know that she took in Paul and Silas after they had been jailed, she made the leap of faith to embrace Christianity, and her house may have served as a center for Christian work. Each of these decisions was risky on her part but also part and parcel of the entrepreneurial spirit she surely possessed.

Being brave requires faith, and having faith requires bravery. What does the Bible urge us to do, again and again, in the face of fear? To trust in the Lord. God gave every parent the capacity for bravery. But true godly bravery means living according to what God alone tells us. That means putting our faith in God and putting His plans for us and our family first, above anything else.

Your own version of "brave" probably doesn't look the same as anybody else's. Homeschooling may scare some parents and delight others. Having one child may be overwhelming to some, while having six or seven is another person's limit. Being courageous is not about seeking sameness but simply about seeking. It's also about pushing away envy and jealousy over things that have nothing to do with you. That exercise requires you to be brave with your life.

These days, every friend, family member, or follower has an opinion on what you show the world. But when one person steps into their calling with courage, they pave the way for others to follow. An act of courage is a bold move forward that can make life uncomfortable, if only for a while, for anybody who undertakes it—but it is a move forward.

 PRAYER

God, I believe that if You command something in the Bible, then You give us the capacity to obey. So when You call us to courage, You know that we are capable! Parenting can be scary, but You are our peace. I trust You as I continue forward bravely in parenthood.

GOD IS SUFFICIENT FOR YOU

My grace is sufficient for you,
for My strength is made perfect in weakness.
II CORINTHIANS 12:9 NKJV

f you've ever Googled anything, you've discovered that the world is filled with overwhelming—and often contradictory—information. Simply choose one topic that parents wonder about: potty training, for example. Type it into a search engine and watch the advice flow: "If you haven't started by eighteen months, you've scarred your child for life!" "Children aren't ready until they're three years old!" "Use the big toilet!" "Use a potty chair!" "Use training pants!" "Go with no pants for the first two days!" It's both exhausting and confusing for new parents.

If you're a normal human being, chances are, you have second-guessed your parenting. And chances are, you will never stop. It's highly unlikely that there will ever be a time when the clouds part, the music soars, and you think, "I've arrived! This is it! I have it *all* figured out, I am the *perfect parent*! Ta *daaaa!*" No matter how hard you work, how gentle or firm, scheduled or relaxed, consistent or gracious, fun-loving or militant you are, achieving perfection as a parent is impossible.

34

That may sound hopeless. But raising kids doesn't require perfection. It requires grace—grace for your children, other parents, and yourself. It can be hard to accept grace for parenting because it is important—and highly emotional. We carry these babies for nine long months, stroking our bellies and promising ourselves that we will never raise our voices, always be patient, and make all the right decisions. Then they're born, small and helpless, and the questions start rolling around in our heads.

The funny thing about grace is, the more you realize you need it, the more you are able to give it to other people. Becoming a mother often softens the heart toward our own parents and the faults we perceived them as having. From the perspective of the roller coaster called parenthood, we can more easily recognize when someone else is just trying their very best. And that is good enough, because grace covers us all.

 PRAYER

Your grace is more than enough, God, and
Your power is made perfect in my weakness.
I surrender my desire for perfection and
accept Your gift of excellence—which involves
seeking You and following Your lead
as I parent my children.

TRUST GOD

LOVE JESUS

AND

WASH YOUR HANDS

SOMEONE IS PRAYING FOR YOU

Come near to God and
He will come near to you.
JAMES 4:8 NIV

Parenthood comes in a blur of emotion. It's awe at the tiny miracle wrapped in your arms. It's overwhelm at all there is to learn and the incredible importance of keeping a baby person alive under your watch. It can be loneliness—of navigating new parenthood without the help of family ... or of being the only one in your age group with a baby. It can be desperation at translating the cries of a newborn or at needing more than four hours of sleep each night. It can also be joy—so much joy, interspersed between the hard—bursting like fireworks as your baby smiles for the first time or learns to sit up or eats her first spoonful of peas.

Nobody, repeat that: *nobody* knows how to parent before they become parents. All the observation in the world, all the social media experts, all the advice in books or over the phone cannot prepare a parent for *their* child. Because your journey is your own, it can feel so isolated. And those feelings can be exacerbated by well-meaning people assuring you that time flies, and to enjoy it while you can, and just wait until she's a teenager or flying the coop.

But you can find confidence in this: there *are* people praying for you. Jesus Himself is before the throne of the Father, speaking on your behalf. Your prayers matter to Him. He knows what isolation and overwhelm feel like. And He will be the first to tell you, this is a season. An important season that is growing you, maturing you, enriching you, and blessing you in ways beyond anything you can imagine right now.

There are times in life when we walk more by faith than others. The foggy, sleepless, strange, new parenthood time is one of them. Be blessed, and know that this time will soon become one of the richest memories you'll carry for the rest of your life.

 PRAYER

Father, I will remember that
You see me even when I feel invisible.
I will wake up each day with the hope of
feeling You near, partnering with me
as I learn to parent this tiny gift.

YOU CAN DO IT

He will not let you stumble; the One
who watches over you will not slumber.
PSALM 121:3 NLT

[ach morning, you tie up your laces and step
outside. You strap the oldest child into the
front stroller seat, and the middle child into
the rear and then dole out an abundance of
snacks and sippy cups. You pray that their
wiggly bodies will calm under the security of
the Houdini-like harnesses. Then you hoist
the baby into the strappy apparatus attached
to your chest. Tiny sun hat and pacifier—
check. Burp cloth tucked into your back
pocket in case the morning's projectile spit-
up isn't quite finished—check. You are ready
to go.

Your feet pound the pavement as you strain
to propel the precious cargo forward. You
push harder, trying to relieve the pressure
that presses from the inside. You are out of
breath before you make it to the end of the
block. The older two babble to one another
about kitties perched in picture windows
and earthworms squished flat on driveways.
You battle your thoughts. *Just go home!*
You're sleep-deprived and out of shape. Why
torture yourself this way? Turn on the TV for

them and go back to bed. But then you hear, *No, you need this. Stay the course. You'll find your rhythm. It will get easier. Just breathe.*

Sanity is a good thing. You turn toward the foothills aglow with morning light and make your way to the quaint Main Street just coming alive. Shop owners turn on lights; hot coffeepots steam as waitresses in maroon aprons fill mugs for customers huddled around small sidewalk tables. The wobbly left stroller wheel clunks hard over another concrete bulge. The baby kicks his legs and a tiny sock falls off again. You pause to pick it up, sip some water, and kiss each toddler. You keep pushing north.

Parenthood comes to everyone differently. But it always comes with a way forward. It may feel like slogging with all you've got at times, bearing the weight of your little ones while struggling to breathe. But, friend, know that every step forward is a victory—every moment you are succeeding at loving your children and fulfilling your purpose as a parent. Keep jogging, rickety stroller and all.

☙ ☙ ☙ PRAYER

Thank You, Lord, for being the best jogging partner there is. Lift me up and keep me from stumbling. In Jesus's name, amen.

GOD HEARS YOUR PRAYERS

I cried out to the LORD;
yes, I prayed to my God for help.
He heard me from His sanctuary.
PSALM 18:6 NLT

Our children's lives are changed forever when we pray. God hears our cries. He hears our hearts. Lay your hand on your baby each night while they sleep, praying blessings and hopes, and God hears. Cry out in pain to Him when you see your child making wrong decisions, and He hears. Your heartfelt prayers for protection or of thanks for who your beautiful child is, and is becoming, are heard by God. He delights in them. It strengthens not only your child's life but also your own relationship with God when you pray.

The gap between our lips and God's ears is the shortest distance in all of creation. And not only does He hear us, but I John 5:14–15 reminds us that when we ask according to His will, we have what we've asked for. "God, I want my child to follow You all the days of her life." His will. "Father, comfort my child as he works out a tough problem at school." His will. We cry out, God hears, and He sees to it. We may not always be there, available and able to hold our child's hand through every circumstance. But we can place our child in His hands. Through the peace and comfort of the Holy Spirit, our prayer is more effective than any earthly thing we can do.

Prayer is not a last resort. It's a first line of defense for anything you or your family may go through. Perhaps this is a reason newborns are up at night for feedings and changes? It's an opportunity to put into place the very important habit of praying over your child. There's not much else to do at two in the morning, after all! Use the downtime to focus on the sweetness of your new baby and ask the Lord how to cover your child in prayer. There's literally no better investment you could make from day one.

 PRAYER

*Lord, thank You for designing me
to be stronger through prayer with You,
and thank You that my prayers can effectively
grow my baby into a stronger person for Your
glory. Hold my baby close to Your heart,
and teach me how to pray as effectively
as possible.*

YOU HAVE A PERFECT FATHER

I pray that you, being rooted
and firmly established in love,
may be able to comprehend with
all the saints what is the length and width,
height and depth of God's love.
EPHESIANS 3:17–18 CSB

f you ever find yourself dropping off a child at a nursery, you're likely to witness a form of fear and anxiety in some of the children there. Sobs may erupt as little ones start to realize they can't see their parents. Some little ones remain inconsolable until their parents return and take them back into their arms. Fortunately, as children mature, they gain a greater understanding of their parents' reliability and deep commitment to them and can learn to step away from their fears.

It's not unlike how we walk through our relationship with God. Over and over again on our journey, fear and anxiety can rule as we face unknown situations. Take new parenthood, for example. So many things we haven't experienced before, so much responsibility seemingly dropped into our lap—it can be a lot like the first day of school for us! And depending on the day, it can very much feel as if He has already abandoned us or will if we make the wrong move. It's the mindset of an infant who doesn't understand the situation. As His beloved children, we are never on the brink of abandonment, despite what our feelings tell us. In fact, even when we feel like God has left and He's out of our sight, especially when we veer off His prescribed path, His sovereign hand is still holding us. Before the world was even created, God devised a plan through faith in His Son that would pave a permanent path back to Him no matter what problem besets us.

Parenthood often brings up a lot of emotions and memories from our growing-up years. But we can let the panic, shame, misunderstanding, and fear of our younger years go. We are being held right in this moment. We have a loving Father, our heavenly Daddy, who has made a way for us to belong to Him forever, and He will never leave us, nor will He forsake us.

 PRAYER

Father, You model perfect parenthood for me.
Lead me as I embark on this path
with my own babies.

RELISH YOUR MOMENTS

Children are a gift from the Lord;
they are a reward from Him.
PSALM 127:3 NLT

Before you know it, you'll look back and wonder where the time went. It will all seem like a flash of diaper changing, nursing, potty training, first days of school, holidays, birthdays, and summer breaks. Amid all the highlights and memories will be the ordinary, everyday days ... the ones when it seems that no one slept through the night or everyone forgot their homework or lunch ... when naptime is held as carefully as gold and bedtime is secretly anticipated. Because even though you love your kids with every fiber of your being, for heaven's sake, a small break just to think without interruptions would be stellar. You'll remember that moment when you looked into the eyes of your child and felt that you couldn't love him or her more, only to find out a few minutes later that he or she had managed to destroy something you thought was unbreakable. While you were in that luxurious three-minute shower.

Every season of parenthood carries its own challenges. But it will fly. The very best thing to do is to savor every moment as much as you are able. Relish the sweet, quiet times, the rowdy, fun times, the hard, grumpy times. Because simply having those times means that you have children—gifts from the Lord, truly.

And you know what? You've got this; the Lord is on your side. There is no need to be afraid. God has gifted this child or these children to you and He will never leave you to do it all alone. Your reward is in heaven. While you can't know the full effect you are having on each child each day, the efforts you are making to parent well do not go unnoticed by your heavenly Father. He loves your babies even more than you do, and He loves the work you are doing to raise them well. Love on. Pray on. Heaven is going to be such an incredible revelation.

 PRAYER

God, there is so much ahead that I don't know
about yet. But with You, it will be fun.
It will be possible. It will be hard and
amazing and wonderful. Go before me
to make a way, and I'll follow You
on this adventure of parenthood!

YOU CAN EXPECT THE BEST

But those who wait on the Lord shall renew
their strength; they shall mount up with wings
like eagles, they shall run and not be weary,
they shall walk and not faint.
ISAIAH 40:31 NKJV

It's common, when a woman is pregnant, to hear someone refer to her as "expecting." From the moment you see that little pink line on a pregnancy test, you have a sense that *this is definitely happening.* "Expecting" parents paint nurseries, buy diapers, attend showers, and announce genders. They post ultrasound pictures, deliberate over names, and plan family visits. Life shifts when parents are "expecting."

According to Webster's 1828 dictionary, to *expect* is to wait for or to look for something. The implication is that the "something" is definitely coming ... something in the future, something already promised. And it's true that being pregnant feels very much like a promise. A baby, growing unseen for nine months, emerges as the most life-changing bundle a parent could ever imagine. It's almost as if God says, every time a baby is born, "See, I told you I'm in the miracle business."

Babies are the most tangible example of how God births new things through us all of the time. He gives us dreams, plants the seeds, waters them with time and experience, and allows them to grow to maturity before releasing them into the world. He gives us the tools to live out the vision He has cast for us. We learn, we work with Him, and His glory is revealed.

Whatever God is birthing in you, a baby will only make it a richer, more tangible experience. Expect the very best from God in the coming months and years. Prepare yourself for whatever dreams He's been whispering into your heart. Clean up your schedule, tell people you trust, and think hopefully and joyfully about what He's unfolding in and through you. He's been planning on this time in your life since time began. In a way, as you wait on Him and expect His very best, He is waiting on you and expecting the great things He has already planned.

PRAYER

God, I have no reason to doubt the plans You have for me. As I lock into parenthood, I also look forward to all that You are doing in me and in my family, for Your glory.

It is not that we are competent in ourselves
to claim anything as coming from ourselves,
but our adequacy is from God.
II CORINTHIANS 3:5 CSB

You are not alone in the important endeavor of parenting. You may feel as if you're alone. You may not have a partner or a supportive family. You may live far away from those who could offer hands-on help and encouragement. But God is with you wherever you are in, whatever you're facing. He is faithful, and He will see you through.

If you're drowning in your circumstances, trust that the Lord is there to help you. Push away the panic and acknowledge that He knows what He's doing. Once you relax and let Him take over, you'll be surprised at how quickly life feels manageable again. Worry is a drain on your precious reserves of time, energy, and emotional strength. How much better it is to talk over those worries with God and let Him keep watch.

You don't have to know everything there is to know about being a parent. Promise. God has placed certain instincts within you, instincts that surface once you relax and let them flow naturally. You're already more equipped than you think. And it's important to remember that God made you. That's right, you are His creation, and He knows you inside out and backward. If you need strength after a long night, He will bolster you. If you need insight, He's the fountain of all baby knowledge. Sometimes He will provide what you need by sending someone your way, and sometimes He will help you reach deep inside and find what you need to get the job done.

Being a new parent can be stressful under any circumstances, but at the same time, it is a time you will deeply cherish as you look back. You will be able to experience it just once with the child you are now holding. Be comforted by the Bible, God's Word, and allow Him to help you enjoy every moment.

 PRAYER

Guide me in Your truth, Lord.
Lead me to the Scriptures that best capture
Your heart for me in this season
so that I can remain strong as a parent
and as Your child.

YOU CAN TRUST GOD

"I am the Lord's servant. May everything you have said about me come true."

LUKE 1:38 NLT

Mary was engaged. She was a virgin. And she was pregnant. With the Messiah. As a devout Jewish girl, there was nothing usual—or acceptable—about her situation. "An angel said I'm carrying God's Son" probably didn't quell the angry masses. Mary was most certainly surrounded by skeptics and furious family members. Not to mention a very confused Joseph, her fiancé.

But as far as the Bible reflects, Mary didn't allow her senses, or those of the people around her, to dictate her heart's position. Her *stance* was to trust in the Lord, even when her *circum*stance (her situation) was intense. Mary chose to believe her God when He said it would all be okay.

"Be still, and know that I am God!" (Psalm 46:10 NLT). In the Hebrew translation of this verse, you'll find the word *yadá* as the translation for "know." The word can refer to knowing through observation or experience. But *yadá* also carries with it a sense of direct, intimate contact. Elsewhere in the Bible, the word is used to refer to a husband and wife knowing each other in the most intimate earthly sense. When referring to the Lord, *yadá* can mean going into the deepest, most personal spaces with Him. God invites us into the very center of His heart.

Mary looked past her surroundings and made choices in line with God's heart for her, for His Son, and for the eternal story of His kingdom. To do this, she lived out Proverbs 3:5–6 on a daily basis: to trust in God, to rely on Him alone, to know the depths of His heart, and to let Him lead her. It was this lifestyle of intimacy with Him that allowed her to give a wise answer in the time of greatest need.

As a new parent, you may be facing your own sort of emotional or familial challenges. But like Mary, you are invited into the depth of relationship with God that allows you to trust Him on the most intimate level. He's never afraid to hear your innermost thoughts. And if you share them, it will only go well for you.

 PRAYER

God, help me to lean on You and not on my own understanding. In all my ways, I will acknowledge You so that You can make my path straight.

# YOU ARE NORMAL

He said to me, "My grace is sufficient for you,
for My power is perfected in weakness."
II CORINTHIANS 12:9 CSB

She was having a hard time with the day-to-day of life. She had two little ones and was pregnant. She felt very lonely, she was overwhelmed, and she suffered from guilt that she wasn't doing enough or being a good enough wife, mother, employee, or homemaker.

She tried explaining to her husband that she felt as if she were drowning and he was asking her to swim harder, when what she needed was for him to pull her out of the water. He worked all day and she was alone with three babies. But he worked all day. And then he had to come home and relieve her, and he needed a break sometimes too. In some ways, he was drowning as well. The days with little ones and out-of-control hormones were dark water days. She felt very alone and very, very tired.

If you are experiencing a season where life feels under water and you are gasping for breath, you are not alone. Others have been there and are there now. You feel crazy, emotional, tired, and overwhelmed, and you're not sure whether you can ask for help. You don't want to be a burden. But you're not okay. Neither are you crazy. Facebook statuses and blog posts where everyone's children are happy and cute are just the pretty side of the painting. The art is beautiful, but creating it is messy and time-consuming and painstaking. Everyone's children yell. Everyone's children has conflict. Everyone's children spill milk, pee in their bed, and ask a million questions when the parent's head is about to explode. And sometimes, we do explode. Cut yourself some slack. You are normal. You are kind of a mess (but not *all* mess). You will come out of this season. The shore is just a few more waves away.

 PRAYER

*Father, I know that the hard days will come
and that I will get through them.
Thank You for Your grace to handle it
and Your mercy when I don't handle it well.*

YOU ARE SEEN

*See what great love the Father
has lavished on us, that we should
be called children of God!*
I JOHN 3:1 NIV

You are a parent in your own unique way. No one parents exactly like you, and for that reason, you are uniquely suited to parent your child. You are the knower of small things, of favorites and things not-so-loved. You can empower with a word. You can heal with a hug. You can calm with a look. At times, you struggle to find power and purpose in what you do, feeling unimportant and unimpressive. It's easy to look for affirmation that may never come from your spouse, kids, coworkers, or friends. It's a good thing we have a God who adores and affirms parents.

We have a God who sees parenthood as a valuable calling and, in His wisdom, gifts us individually. He delights in you personally. He has paired you and prepared you, equipped you and called you, and dressed you in His finest armor to face the day with joy. You have no idea how much you influence your world.

God. Delights. In. You. Yep, you. You, who are weary. You, who are a parent to children not of your blood. You, in the office cubicle. You, who diligently serves on church committees or community groups. You, who loves being a parent. You are beloved to Him. God delights in His children. The end.

When you feel the weight of not knowing whether you make a difference ... when you feel the tedium of another day of the same things ... when you feel the heat of trying to do the very best you can for your family ... God sees it all and reassures you: "Count it all joy, child. I see you. I know you. I can't wait for you to feel the warmth of My acceptance of you in all its fullness. In the meantime, take comfort in the peace that passes understanding. You are right where you belong—in this home, with this family, and in My heart."

PRAYER

It's easy to lose sight of the incredible gift of Your love, Lord—especially in the mire of everyday life. The enemy tries to keep us foggy and unsure. But I know that You are right behind me, clear as day, saying, "This is the way—walk in it." Fight for my family, Lord, as You promised.

GOD IS YOUR SHEPHERD

He tends His flock like a shepherd:
He gathers the lambs in His arms and
carries them close to His heart;
He gently leads those that have young.
ISAIAH 40:11 NIV

As new parents, the words of Isaiah 40:11 hold special significance. What amazing comfort we can accept, knowing that God gently gathers us in His strong arms and carries us close to His own heart as we care for our babies. As new parents, we often feel insecure, wondering what on earth we are doing caring for this helpless little child in the "unknown," as there is no real training for what is to come. Let this verse encourage you and give you hope that God Himself will lead you in this new journey.

One interesting thing about this passage is that if you read the surrounding verses, in verse 10, it states that the "Lord comes with power, and He rules with a mighty arm" (NIV). Then in verse 11, we learn that that same strong arm is used to gently swoop us up and carry us so tenderly. Everything we need from a perfect Father and powerful Shepherd, we can find in God.

Mama sheep, when they see a stranger, will immediately start guarding their babies and bleating. They will protect their young from danger—but soften entirely when the familiar farmer comes. The sheer sound of his voice puts them at ease. They know they are safe. They will even allow you close to their most treasured possessions, their babies.

God is our good Shepherd. His sheep know His voice. He gently cares for His young. He protects and guides them. He nourishes them. So, as new parents, we can be doubly blessed— in knowing that He is perfectly leading us and in knowing that He is gently caring for our babies even as we care for them. There's no need to fear that we aren't enough. We can relax in Jesus, knowing that we're covered from every angle.

PRAYER

Thank You, Jesus, Shepherd to new parents and to babies. We shall not want. Surely goodness and mercy will follow us all the days of our lives, and we will dwell in Your house forever.

YOUR CHILD IS A GIFT FROM GOD

*Whoever welcomes one little child
such as this in My name welcomes Me.*
MARK 9:37 CSB

In some ways, life gets more complicated with a baby. Free time is no longer your own. Logistics and schedules become a way of life. But in other ways, a baby changes everything for the simpler. There's something downright spiritual about snuggling a newborn asleep on your chest. And you have no choice but to go at the speed of your baby's development—with eating, with diapers, with tummy time and rolling over and giggles and all the milestones we've been trained to look for. With a baby in the picture, we begin to see life in its infancy again. When everything feels new to us, and everything *is* new for the tiny human we're in charge of, we somehow begin to unhinge from habits and expectations. Our world gets a little smaller—at least for a while—as we focus on what's right in front of us.

There's no mistake that God has designed babies to need us for absolutely everything. He surely knew, when He organized life, that adults would need to be shaken out of their know-it-all stupor from time to time. He knew that we would need to be reminded to slow down and see the simplicity of pure trust. Because babies grow, they become more independent, but they still turn to their parents for help and support. They instinctively know that they need Mama or Daddy and can count on them. And as we watch our little ones discover our love for them, we get to relate it to God's love for His own children.

God loves children. He feels very strongly about them—about protecting them, guiding them in His way, and loving them with His whole heart. When He entrusts us with a baby, He gives us a part of Himself. So when we sit with our babies, we would do well to marvel at what He's given us: the proof that He loves us beyond measure and thinks a lot about our ability to care for what He cares so strongly and passionately for.

PRAYER

Father, Your love for me is overwhelming,
and I can feel it through the gift of my baby.
I commit to loving this child as purely and as
deeply as I possibly can, shepherding this gift
You've given with my whole heart.

YOU WERE MADE FOR COMMUNITY

That's how it is with us. There are many of us,
but we each are part of the body of Christ,
as well as part of one another.
ROMANS 12:5 CEV

Looking into the eyes of your newborn, a gift without instructions, you may come to realize that you just can't do it alone. Despite the support of your spouse or the wisdom of others whose babies are grown, you may feel an ache of loneliness.

You may find that you need someone else to look you in the eyes and say, "I didn't sleep last night either." Or someone to show up at your house in a spit-up-stained shirt. Then you could point to your own shirt (the one you slept in two nights in a row), and you could commiserate together. You might be craving the companionship of others with whom you can walk down the road of first-time parenthood. There's just something about facing the same fears in the same moment with people who really see you. If this is you, then pray, *Lord Jesus, please bring me friends.* And He will.

In between the diaper changes, the feedings, the shushing, the exhaustion, and the joy, friendship will form. Joined hearts will always walk life together, making it stronger. That's what friendship does. We were never meant to travel this life without the refuge of our friends. Life is messy and painful.

Life lived in relationship allows us to survive the deep end. We can test the waters alone and wade out a bit by ourselves, but if we must head to the deep places of life, we need friends to keep the ocean from swallowing us whole. Each friendship can serve as a line, tethering us to the shore when life tries to suck us under.

In His great mercy and grace, our Jesus has given us the gift of friendship. And if you're in the space, ankle-deep and headed toward the dark waters, pray for hands to hold you. Pray and ask our Holy One for kindred spirits to walk beside you in this journey. The drowning only comes when we attempt to travel alone.

PRAYER

Lord, You know what I need most during this season. Please bring me a friend who will fill any gaps, and help me to walk this season of life in beautiful community.

YOU CAN RESPOND IN LOVE

But God chose the foolish things
of this world to put the wise to shame.
He chose the weak things of this world
to put the powerful to shame.
I CORINTHIANS 1:27 CEV

At some time or another, we are all faced with how to respond to an insult—especially as a new parent, when child-rearing philosophies become full-blown arguments or, at the very least, snobby down-the-nose looks from disdainful passersby. Whether from another parent, a spouse, a child, or a total stranger, we've all been talked down to or felt disrespected.

Our lives are full of small-scale snubs, which is why they add up to a lot. The accumulation of these little injuries, along with our responses to them, says a lot about us. They are a testimony of sorts. In I Corinthians 4:10 Paul refers to believers as "fools for Christ." Paul knew a thing or two about looking foolish, and he even seemed comfortable with the label. Why? Because he didn't care about his reputation. He only cared about Christ's. As long as Jesus got the glory, Paul couldn't have cared less about what anyone thought. If anything, God's ability to use a "fool" like him was an even greater testimony to His might.

Remember that our reputation matters little, but Christ's matters much. Remember that in our silence, we choose to be a "fool for Christ." Remember that sometimes God uses the "foolish" to teach the "wise" (I Corinthians 1:27). And remember that Christ looked foolish, bearing insults gladly, just for us. It's hard to be a fool for Christ, but it's also liberating. There is nothing better than walking away from a conflict knowing that you honored your Savior. Insults sting for a little while, but the delight of the Lord is such freedom. True joy comes not from our own glittering reputation, but from a life spent pointing the world to His.

Look at your sweet little one, her weaknesses and helplessness, and remember that you have what it takes. You, your baby, and Jesus are going to do just fine.

♭ ♭ ♭ PRAYER

Father, when people have opinions about
my parenting, help me to respond in love.
When the "haters" point their venom toward
me or my family, I will do my very best
to make sure it's You they see—
not the world through me.

EVERY GOOD
AND PERFECT GIFT
IS FROM ABOVE.
JAMES 1:17 NIV

YOU WON'T MISS A THING

*Every good gift and every perfect gift is
from above, and comes down from the Father.*
JAMES 1:17 NKJV

There's one thing about becoming a new parent that no one talks about much: the time warp. Somehow, once a new baby enters the picture, time utterly slows down in your home—while it speeds up everywhere else. Just watch social media: the world moves on, your friends start having all the fun, the new smartphone comes out, stand-up paddleboarding becomes all the rage, and the best movies hit the theaters. Meanwhile, you're home. Holding a baby. Feeding a baby. Changing a baby. Burping a baby. Trying to get a shower. Over. And over. And over again. Every day. All night. Sure, having a baby is *wonderful*. But at the same time, your house suddenly seems to enter the movie *Groundhog Day*, while everyone else is having the time of their lives. Certainly the term FOMO ("fear of missing out") was birthed out of a home with a new baby.

But catch that truth up there about three-fourths of the way through the paragraph: having a baby is *wonderful*. It's a gift. And if it's a gift from God (which it most certainly is), then having a baby brings benefits beyond compare. Maybe—just maybe—it's the world that misses out. Maybe the world needs to sit down and stick its nose into the soft folds of a newborn's neck. Maybe the world needs to run its lips gently across tiny baby toes. Maybe the world needs to take the week off and spend each afternoon with its arms holding a seven-pound sleeper on its chest, feeling the quick little breaths and listening to those soft coos of the freshest, most innocent dreams.

Maybe the world has forgotten how to relish life. And maybe you, with your newly arranged schedule and perfectly sweet little person in your arms, are the stuff of envy. And maybe the world knows it. Maybe the world will try to convince you to be more like *it*, when you have every right to whisper from your rocking chair, "Come and sit. Enjoy this moment. Really, *really* enjoy it. Don't let it slip past unnoticed."

 PRAYER

*I know that if I blink, I'll miss it all, Lord—
the newness of life and gift You've given
this family. Remind me as often as needed
that this time is precious.*

GOD KNOWS YOUR BABY

He counts the number of the stars;
He gives names to all of them.
PSALM 147:4 CSB

One of the most blessed realizations that a new parent comes to is that their baby is already a person. That is not a realization, you say. That is obvious! But it's easy for us, as the earthly people fully responsible for our little ones, to forget that God is actually the one in charge. He already formulated your baby's DNA. He programmed body type, likes and dislikes, gifts and talents, and so much more. Your baby doesn't need to be built from the ground up. Your baby needs parents who will observe the person God created him or her to be. Babies need parents who will champion their strengths, love through their weaknesses, and train them to fix their eyes on Jesus.

That is *not* to minimize the work of a parent in the life of a child. Parents make an infinite number of decisions that will affect their baby's growth and development. But the primary role of a parent is to love their baby— and pray.

Pray that your baby will know God on the

deepest level. Pray that as your baby grows, he or she will hold strong to the truths of the kingdom of heaven. Ask God how to pray for your baby, and follow His lead. You'll find that having a baby is one of the best opportunities for your own growth in the Lord!

Your baby is a person who has been meticulously planned by the Maker of the universe. He designed the color of their eyes to go with the shape of their face. He appointed that smile, those fingers, those wisps of hair. Instead of worrying, spend your time marveling at the creation in your lap. And marvel at the fact that God is asking you to partner with Him to raise up this little one.

You yourself were chosen by God, loved by Him, and designed in great detail. He knew your name before you were even a thought in your parents' minds. Likewise, your baby is just as loved and known.

 PRAYER

Father, thank You for creating
such a marvel that I get to call my child.
I love Your marvelous handiwork! I know that
You are with me every step of the way
and that You won't lead me wrong.

GOD IS YOUR REFUGE

Trust in Him at all times ... pour out
your hearts before Him. God is our refuge.
PSALM 62:8 CSB

Be a parent for any time at all and you'll have the need to trust God. But with so much "new" already, it probably won't be on the top of your mind to turn to God in every circumstance. Especially if you have more than one munchkin to manage! When the baby is screaming because she just woke up hungry and the toddler escaped from the bathroom before a bath and has—well—enjoyed his diaperless freedom in a most inconvenient way, then yelling, screaming, crying, catching, cleaning, and feeding are all responses competing with "crying out to God." When your five-month-old wakes up with his first fever in the middle of the night and won't be consoled, your tired brain may just panic or worry before turning to the Lord in prayer. Or some days, when all the everythings are crumbling around you for no good reason... Chin up. Take heart. Turn to God. Remember... He can be trusted.

God has equipped you for everything in your path. If He hasn't equipped you for something, then He won't allow it to come your way. In that, you can trust.

Nothing happens that God hasn't foreseen. He's never knocked off-balance by some unexpected drama. In that, you can trust.

When you're aching, tired, lonely, scared, confused, and at your wit's end, God is already there to comfort you and show you the way out. Sometimes that just means a nap and a cup of coffee and, if so, then He's already enlisted someone to make sure that happens for you. In that, you can trust.

While He knows it all, God still wants you to tell Him. He makes space for you to cry out to Him simply so that He can show you how much He cares. He wants to hear your heart.

The "new parent" season doesn't last forever, even though there are moments it feels like things will never change. And remember... *the "new parent" season doesn't last forever*. These are moments you will never get back. So trust God. At all times. Pour out your heart, and allow Him to be your refuge.

 PRAYER

God, thank You for hearing me. I trust You.
I will turn to You in need and thanks
and joy. Amen.

GOD WILL GIVE YOU REST

*Come to Me, all you who are weary
and burdened, and I will give you rest.*
MATTHEW 11:28 NIV

There's no doubt about it and no way around it: if you have a new baby, you do not have enough time in your day for the amount of sleep you would like to have. Perhaps it's a way the Lord has designed us to be broken down for parenthood.

Being a parent means being tested in every single selfish area of our lives. Our tiny new person demands more from us than we are likely comfortable giving. But if we let it, that breaking down can be a beautiful thing. We learn as we go. We find that eating second, showering when possible, doing our online shopping for the next size of clothes and diapers instead of the next new thing in handbags—these are all ways we can surrender more to the process of life. In some ways, parenting means learning to stop fighting for what we used to have and start embracing a new way of looking at what we have now.

Don't feel badly if you struggle with losses: lost free time, lost availability, lost sleep, lost hobbies. After all, those things are not really lost, just reallocated. Watch for them to resurface in due course. Also, don't feel badly if you haven't mastered the surrender by your baby's first birthday! We are human. Which means that we will be fighting imperfection until death do us part from all our worldly comforts and preferences. Instead, watch for the subtle changes. Watch for the sense of peace that comes when you're up at two a.m. and rocking your little one back to sleep. Watch for your gentle responses to a tired toddler. Watch for the laughs you share with your spouse over a poorly timed diaper change. As many ways as we are apt to be selfish, there are just as many ways the Lord works through us when we come to Him—wearily, but willingly—and let Him do the work.

✿ ✿ ✿ PRAYER

*Lord, I am weary of trying to do things
the way I thought they should be done.
I surrender to You—minute by minute
if I have to—until You have Your way
in me and my family.*

YOUR WORDS BLESS YOUR BABY

I will bless you and make your descendants
into a great nation. You will become famous
and be a blessing to others.
GENESIS 12:2 CEV

There's evidence all over the Old and New Testaments that blessing others with mouths and hearts is a regular practice in the kingdom of God. But what does that mean exactly? And how does it affect our kids? Sometimes we think of blessings as tangible things. "This new car is a real blessing." "I'll ask God to bless you with good health." But in reality, a blessing is more accurately a pronunciation of happiness or an act of praise. God's blessings bring happiness to us, and we can pronounce a wish of happiness over others. God is also blessed when we praise Him.

There are two major ways that we can bless our children. The first is one that we can do from the day they are born. A blessing over your baby while they sleep in their crib may sound something like this:

"May you always know the sound of your Shepherd Jesus's voice. May you truly love following Him on your path through life. May your body stay strong, your mind stay steadfast, and your heart seek the very best for you and the world around you. May you grow in wisdom and knowledge. And may your children's children find favor in the eyes of the Lord."

It may seem strange to speak to your baby when you're certain he or she can't yet understand. But when we bless, we aren't necessarily speaking to their minds. We are spiritual beings, after all. A blessing, delivered on the wings of the Holy Spirit, is a gift to the spirit of a person. You have the ability to pronounce happiness over your baby even while he or she is still in the womb. God was speaking to us while we were still growing inside our mothers (Isaiah 49:1). Even before that, the Bible tells us, God knew us by name (Jeremiah 1:5).

Every word of kindness and happiness that you speak over your baby will take root. It will grow as your baby grows. And it will bear fruit. We don't always know how that fruit will manifest—but your words, without a doubt, will have a positive effect.

PRAYER

God, I want the very best for my baby.
Teach me to speak words of life over this child.

I will go before you and
level the uneven places.
ISAIAH 45:2 CSB

If there's one thing a new parent can do with great proficiency, it's worry! Many late nights, little sleep, so much *new*, and so much *love* make up a great recipe for thinking up the reasons catastrophe might befall your baby throughout her lifetime. It's amazing where a mind can go in the middle of the night. *Will she marry a good man? Will he find a career that satisfies him? What if she falls and breaks a bone? What if he decides to turn from God?* The list is endless. It's a hamster wheel of hopelessness that could truly take up every waking minute, if we weren't spending most of our time kissing chubby cheeks and bathing tiny bums.

When things of the future get scary in your mind, remember Isaiah 45:2: God promises to go before you and level the uneven places. He will make a way forward—for you and for your baby. That doesn't mean that life will be perfect and painless. But God does promise to go with you (Exodus 33:14). He promises never to leave you, never to forsake you (Hebrews

13:5). He promises that if you seek Him, He will be found (Jeremiah 29:13). And that if you train up your child in the way he should go, then when he is old, he won't depart from it (Proverbs 22:6).

God promises that if you pray and ask, with thanksgiving, then His peace (the kind that it doesn't make sense to have, considering the circumstances) will guard your heart and your mind in Christ Jesus (Philippians 4:6–7). When your mind starts going down the path that leads to anxiety, then speak to your mind. Remind it that all those horrible things haven't happened and they most likely never will happen. But whatever *does* happen, God will give you the grace for it. And He'll go through it with you. Right now, instead of worrying, start marveling—at this moment, with your sweet baby. Don't let the future steal from your present. Be present.

 PRAYER

God, I know You'll go with me through
whatever my baby and I face.
And I believe I can peacefully live
in this moment, with joy and expectation
for the good things to come. Help me
to remember Your truth when I need it.

YOU ARE GROWING

For I am confident of this very thing,
that He who began a good work among you
will complete it by the day of Christ Jesus.
PHILIPPIANS 1:6 NASB

New parent, know this: you are doing *great*.
No ... really. Those aren't just some words on
a printed page meant for many people. Those
words were just for you. Because if you're
reading this, you're obviously interested in
growing as a parent, growing in God, and
growing up your child strong.

You are on a one-of-a-kind journey. When
you put yourself in His hands, He will break
you down where needed and build you up
even stronger than before. When you receive
the gift of the Holy Spirit, He will shape you
into someone looking more and more like
Jesus Himself. As you press in, listening for
His voice, surrendering parenthood and your
child to Him, releasing fears and problems
into His hands, you are going down a path
that will perfect you. You are a new creation
spiritually, just as your baby is a new creation
altogether!

God has the whole picture, and He knows
exactly where you fit. For some reason, this

little baby of yours fits perfectly into His plan for your life. Your baby is here to grow and learn and impact the world for the glory of God. But ... *so are you*. Parenting isn't just about your child. Parenting is a means by which God will shape you into His image.

It's completely normal to feel inadequate at times as you raise your little one. But Jesus lifts you up, strengthens you, and makes the impossible, well, fun! You're definitely growing. But, fortunately, it's impossible to *out*grow Jesus. You need Him now, when your baby is little. And you'll need Him when your preteen has problems at school. You'll need Him when your young adult leaves for college. You'll need Him through all the ups and downs of loving someone with the biggest love imaginable.

You need Him on this journey ... and He's not going anywhere. He will continue to do good work in you until the day of Christ Jesus.

 PRAYER

Father, You have all of me to do with as You see fit. Thank You for doing Your good work in me. I love You!

GOD'S JOY IS YOUR STRENGTH

The lines have fallen to me in pleasant places;
yes, I have a good inheritance.
PSALM 16:6 NKJV

Life is a compare-a-thon—like who can outdo whom with their highlight reel, trying to prove to ourselves (because, really, no one else cares as much as we do) that we measure up to the ideal image of a family.

What if life is more about receiving the joy of the Lord for the situation we've been given? Consider the Israelites in Nehemiah. They had tried for years to rebuild the walls of Jerusalem with no success. Nehemiah was finally able to orchestrate the rebuild. And on the day the people gathered to celebrate, Ezra read Scripture publicly. The people heard all the ways they'd fallen short of God's glory. They wanted to mourn and grieve. But Ezra commanded them not to. He reminded them that it was a day of celebration, asking the people to see the joy of the Lord as their strength (Nehemiah 8:10). Ezra knew that wallowing in their own shortcomings would solve nothing. Instead, he counted on God's joy to sustain them. Calling on joy would cause them to think more like God, serving those who were in need.

Living in joy allows us to see life through God's eyes. Where comparing and envy keep us from moving forward, joy allows us to leap. Joy allows us to love the people we're with. Joy looks past dust or dirty dishes and sees the home that keeps us safe. Joy is what ultimately shines through our posts, making people wonder what makes our family different even though our circumstances may not be picture-perfect.

If you're going to compare, then compare yourself to where you were a year ago. Compare yourself to who you were before you kicked that bad habit or before you chose that new, good habit. Compare life to a few years ago and ask yourself whether you're headed in the right direction. Be thankful for where you are, what God has given, and especially that sweet new life you get to nurture. Then grab onto the joy and keep on going.

✿ ✿ ✿ PRAYER

God, Your joy is my strength and I will live like I mean it! Teach me to choose Your joy over circumstances, whether good or bad. Teach me to find my worth only in what You think of me. In the name of Jesus, amen.

YOU HAVE WISDOM

Now if any of you lacks wisdom, he should ask God—who gives to all generously and ungrudgingly—and it will be given to him.
JAMES 1:5 CSB

Please hear this: you aren't going to mess up your kid. You're such a great parent. You love with a big love, which is what your baby needs most. And if you know God, then you have unlimited resources at your fingertips. Never mind Instagram and expert advice: you have a key to the storehouse of wisdom.

There's definitely a place for listening to expert advice. Many who have degrees or who have gone before can help a parent through the challenges of raising a child. Let's take one example: schooling.

Some veteran parents and experts are of the opinion that homeschooling is the only healthy way to raise a child in this crazy world. Others say that mainstream schooling is the only way to reach the lost—or the best way for a child to learn what the world is like while under the covering of parents' guidance and prayer. Still another view is that private school will offer the best of both worlds. And of course, virtual schooling may be the perfect answer—or possibly the biggest headache—depending on your household. You and your spouse discuss all the options but see benefits and drawbacks to each. You're conflicted. What to do?

God knows the future of your child—and everything else, for that matter. His wisdom can give you insight, even without understanding. As you and your spouse pray together on behalf of your child, and as you listen to His voice, you'll find His wisdom there to point you in a direction that will serve your child, and you, through the schooling process. And when you're in that schooling situation, His wisdom will get you through whatever you face. Hard lessons. Celebrations. Friend choices. Curriculum. All of it lies within the realm of God's wisdom.

Start now to seek His advice, and the rest of the advice will seem so much less daunting. He wants to shepherd you through the most trying of circumstances, with wisdom that will come from no other source.

PRAYER

*Lord, I know that with my child
I'll face all kinds of situations that require
Your wisdom. Thank You for making
Your wisdom available to all who ask.
I will turn to You first, before making
decisions based on worldly information.*

YOU ARE HOME

Do you not know that you are the temple of
God and that the Spirit of God dwells in you?
I CORINTHIANS 3:16 NKJV

Nothing compares to that moment when a baby emerges into the world. No one can prepare you for the myriad emotions that flood in. And few people would debate how amazing it is that a baby grows in a mother's belly. But *why* is it so marvelous? It's happened since the beginning of time. Why hasn't it lost its luster?

One reason that pregnancy and birth awe us so much is because of what they stand for. A pregnancy—whether you're the mother or the father—is an opportunity to experience life in its most spontaneous form. Absolutely nothing apart from the Creator of the universe could cause a person to grow from microscopic cells to a heart-beating, chest-breathing, crying, snuggling, smiling, laughing bundle *from inside another person*. Nothing *we* do can make that growth happen. God shepherds the process from start to finish. Modern medicine allows us to see some of the process through ultrasounds, and a mother experiences all of the ups and downs of her body becoming the vessel a baby needs in order to grow. But, really, we are simply observers in the design God created for life to go on.

And perhaps a baby is so marvelous to us because it's the closest earthly example we have of Christ in us. A baby takes up residence inside her mother until we meet her face to face. And when we choose to follow God, He chooses to take up residence inside of us until we meet Him face-to-face. We can't help but be in awe of this little person who is helpless now but most certainly a world-changer in the making. And we can't possibly understand the incredible fact of God viewing our bodies as His temple as He changes the world through us.

Be encouraged today—the birth of your little one is nothing short of a miracle. And even though your baby may already have left her gestational home, you are still a vessel for the Holy Spirit to work miracles in and through. It's a beautiful thing—and that makes you, well ... beautiful.

 PRAYER

Holy Spirit, You are welcome here.
Do Your work in me, through me, and through
the miracle of my baby. Amen.

YOU HAVE A TRAVEL BUDDY

*He guides the humble in what is right
and teaches them His way.*
PSALM 25:9 NIV

At times in your parenthood journey, the decisions and responsibilities are likely to turn you into a weary traveler who has come to a fork in the road with no map or compass to confirm which way to go. You may feel stranded, abandoned, and unprepared to take a step forward in any direction. What if you make the wrong decision? What if you change your mind? What if you're stuck and can't turn back? What if it's a disaster? What if you fail? You'll pile all the pros and cons and what-ifs into a mountain of anxious uncertainty. Trying to discern what's best for your kids in the face of an ever-changing world can be so tough.

When we're faced with uncertainty, our only certain choice is to turn to Jesus. It's natural to feel the weight of decisions for our kids. It's okay to feel uncertain and stressed. But the key is in believing that you're not alone in making whatever decision you face. God wants to do it with you!

The world doesn't hinge on our ability to

synthesize and analyze incomplete information, perfectly fill in the blanks, and accurately predict the future. We needn't be afraid of making a mistake. Nowhere in God's Word does it say that the world—or parenthood or marriage or next Tuesday—hinges on our ability. Nowhere does Scripture say, "Thou shalt make every decision perfectly and never make a mistake." That's not God's heart for us. So what does Scripture say? God is with us.

"The LORD Himself goes before you and will be with you; He will never leave you nor forsake you. Do not be afraid; do not be discouraged" (Deuteronomy 31:8 NIV). God will guide you. Need more assurance that these things are true? Read Psalm 139. Then be honest with God about where you are. Tell Him if you feel alone or scared, lost or mad or overwhelmed. Then rehearse the truth: "Even there Your hand will lead me; Your right hand will hold on to me" (Psalm 139:10 CSB).

PRAYER

I know You're with me, God.
You're with us as we parent and grow and
learn to follow You. Keep us humble
and focused on the right things.

YOUR QUIET HAS PURPOSE

*Make it your goal to live a quiet life,
minding your own business and
working with your hands.*
I THESSALONIANS 4:11 NLT

The season of new parenting is full of unavoidable daily chores and mundane responsibilities: laundry, feeding, nap times and diapers, finding time for housework, regular work, and marriage work…. You may or may not have dreamed of being a parent. It is a privilege, for sure. But there are bound to be days when you long for more than what your current life offers—perhaps a time and place where you can fully use the gifts and talents you've been given, whatever that might mean.

In I Thessalonians 4, Paul reminds believers to keep living life in a way that pleases God by being holy, by loving others. He's talking about the character and integrity of our faith demonstrated in our lives. How do we build our character and practice integrity? It is worked out in the quiet life, the small life, the daily working of our hands. The hard heart work happens in the dark where no one can see.

There were around eighteen years of darkness or nothingness in Jesus's life about which little is written. Between His time teaching at the temple at twelve years old and the beginning of His ministry at thirty years old, we have only one verse to tell us what happened in those eighteen years. Luke 2:52 says that "Jesus grew in wisdom and in stature and in favor with God and all the people" (NLT). Jesus grew. He was a son, a brother. He lived a normal life and learned his father's trade.

"Mundane" doesn't mean life has no purpose. "Small" and "quiet" are not death sentences to dreams and passions. Instead, those words are simply a different framework in which God is doing His work. This hidden season is fertile ground for Him to strip away what taints our character, to heal our wounds and brokenness, and, most importantly, to tell us again and again that our purpose, our worth, our identity isn't found in accomplishments in life or ministry. Our worth is found in our belovedness, our identity is grounded in Christ, and our purpose is to be like Him.

✧ ✧ ✧ PRAYER

Father, thank You for the quiet season of new parenthood. Do in and through me all that You want to during this time.

GOD IS IN YOUR LONELINESS

If anyone is in Christ, there is a new creation...
everything has become new!
II CORINTHIANS 5:17 NRSV

New parenthood brings a host of new experiences ... one of which can be loneliness. That may be surprising (or maybe affirming, if you're experiencing it now)—but loneliness is a thing. So many new parents lose track of their identity, since everything they did before children is either on hold or done—by necessity—in a completely different way.

We look for something to take away the ache of loneliness. So often we try to resolve our loneliness with social media, wine, online shopping, schedules, a paycheck, or food to fill our deep-down dissatisfaction. But loneliness isn't something to solve. Loneliness becomes the light leading us back to Jesus.

New parenthood doesn't bring about loneliness; it just exposes it. Before children, we could manage our loneliness effortlessly. But now, when there's so much we can't do in the same ways we could before children, God uses parenthood to refine us. He brings up and turns over who we are and reshapes us into those who love radically and without condition.

Through loneliness, God reveals to us all the ways we depended on our capacities instead of His grace. Our loneliness isn't lost on God; it's a means to form us into Christlikeness. He is bending and breaking our character into deeper trust upon His forever love. God is growing you into a new creation.

Loneliness isn't to be feared, pushed aside, or pressed under. Invite it out. Feel its ferocious appetite and the ways you're tempted to fill that hole with anything and everything but God. Let love meet you in the middle of your vulnerable void—the void that Christ knows full well. The place where all the world's weight of loneliness pressed Him to pray, "Why, God, have You forsaken Me?" Meet Christ right there, right where He is always meeting you—arms stretched wide, chest open, love mercifully exposed, welcoming you into a loneliness He fully understands. Your loneliness finds company with Christ, and it leads you back to love and always back to Jesus.

 PRAYER

Lord, meet me in my lonely hours.
Show me what life should look like now
with a baby. Help me understand my role,
and continue to show me patience
as I learn. Amen.

YOU'VE GOT GAME

*You shall love the Lᴏʀᴅ your God
with all your heart, with all your soul,
and with all your strength.*
DEUTERONOMY 6:5 NKJV

Parenting has a way of totally throwing us off our game. We can train for years, even, watching other parents and secretly making mental lists of what we will and won't do when our own offspring come along. Still, when the rubber meets the road—or when the precious little bundle is finally placed in our arms—the game changes. No longer are we idealistic watchers. Our muddy uniforms, banged-up elbows, and exhausted smiles show that, yes, we are finally earning our place in the league of parents. And at that point, all bets are off.

Don't worry; no shame. Life is a balance of all things, and fortunately we have a God who understands. He's had a lot of practice. People in biblical times were often looking for shortcuts too. It seems they were overwhelmed with all the commands given to them by Old Testament living. That's totally understandable, since in the books of the Law (check out Deuteronomy, for example), the list is daunting. Without God's mercy, it was truly impossible not to miss the mark. It stands to reason that if they wanted to honor God, they would want to know exactly how to do that.

And so Jesus was asked the question: "Teacher, which command in the law is the greatest?" (Matthew 22:36 CSB). Jesus responded by quoting Deuteronomy 6:5, followed by Leviticus 19:18: "Love the Lord your God with all your heart, with all your soul, and with all your mind.... The second is like it: Love your neighbor as yourself" (Matthew 22:37–39 CSB).

When it comes down to it, what you need to remember is this: you are loved. You have God's mercy on your side. And if you simply love Him back with everything in you, then He'll lead you through the ups and downs and sidewayses and unknowns and unseens and messes of parenthood. Keep it simple and let God handle the rest.

 PRAYER

Father, teach me to love You with everything I have. Let that be my number-one goal, even above parenting well. When my relationship with You is strong, then I know I'll be stronger in every area of life.

AS YOU HOLD
YOUR BABY,
GOD HOLDS YOU.

GOD TRUSTS YOU

*I chose you. I appointed you to go
and produce fruit and that
your fruit should remain.*
JOHN 15:16 CSB

When you have a baby, you can be sure that you've been appointed to parent a most amazing creature through life. This can be said with certainty because every life is precious to God. He doesn't make mistakes. He doesn't make pairings that could only lead to lousy outcomes. He cares so much about every child ever created, and for that reason you can be sure that He is entrusting you with something very, very special. And the adventure will be something you can never imagine without the experience.

Think of yourself as similar to the parable of the workers in Matthew 25:14–30. The master of the house entrusted three servants with his money while he went away on business. When the master returned, he praised the servants who made wise and thoughtful decisions with his money. He was upset when one servant made a foolish decision out of fear. We don't really know what went on while the master was gone. But for the servants who made wise decisions, they must have invested. They must have spent time researching good options, thinking them through, and keeping tabs on the money. They treated their master's treasure as though it were their own.

On your parenting journey you will likely face fear, and you will definitely face many decisions. But God has empowered you to treat His child (your baby) as your own. After all, your baby will one day be an adult and one day, ultimately, return to the Father. In the meantime, you have a lifetime to invest in your little one and raise him up to bear much fruit.

If your child is a garden, then you are the gardener. You have no control over the power within the seed. But you can help the seed tap into its power. As you watch over her, water and feed her, love her and expose her to the Son; she will most certainly grow. The process will challenge you too. And you'll grow. And both of you will bear much fruit.

PRAYER

*God, thank You for entrusting me
with one of Your most precious gifts.
I commit now to raising my baby to the very
best of my ability, for Your sake. Amen.*

YOU BELONG TO THE REFINER

Create in me a clean heart, O God.
Renew a loyal spirit within me.
PSALM 51:10 NLT

Nothing shines a light on our shortcomings quite like having a child. From the beginning, when our freedom to do whatever we want disappears, on to days when our toddler starts repeating words they hear us say and attitudes they see us display—a child opens our eyes to ourselves in a whole new way.

Losing independence can be scary for some. So can suddenly realizing that your two-year-old pushes the dog away with his feet because he's seen you do it. And your gentle nudge along with "Back up, Rio," coming from a toddler, looks a lot more like a kick. "Bat-uh, Rio!" *Okay*, you think. *Time to examine my methods and adapt them for toddler viewing.* Easy to do when your heart and mind are focused on that one thing in that one moment. But when a million different things are going on and something gets spilled in the kitchen, your usual methods come out for all the pint-sized world to see. *Ugh, I thought I was getting better at this.*

It's a wonder that throughout our entire

0

lives, we fall again and again into the thinking that we can do the hard work without God. Even when He's helped us a thousand times. We need His grace to give us what we're missing. And we need His mercy to free us from what holds us back. We need His healing touch to help us move on and His wisdom to know how to move forward. When little ones enlighten us to areas that need His touch, we need His healing, shaping hands on our heart.

His work is expert. It's the path of least resistance, really. We can try to kick a habit or adapt our methods. But only God can purify the heart, the place where our attitudes, actions, and words are born.

We aren't expected to fix ourselves. We simply need to open ourselves to His work. And even that—the surrender to Him—is a wonderful example we give to our children.

ℭ ℭ ℭ PRAYER

Father, I open myself to You right now.
Do Your refining work in me. As it says
in Psalm 51:10, create in me a clean heart.
Renew a right spirit within me.

GOD IS HERE TO COMFORT YOU

God will tenderly comfort you....
He will give you the strength to endure.
II CORINTHIANS 1:7 TLB

There will be times that you wish had never happened.

There will be days that you want to do over.

There will be moments when you think to yourself, *I'm not strong enough for this.*

It's the way of a parent. To love so deep. So strong. So unfathomable that to see your child hurt will break your heart and threaten to break your spirit.

Along with loving a child comes accepting that there will be heartbreak. It's built into the DNA of that kind of love. Not because we have an evil or vindictive God, but because we're made in His image. And fathering us, for Him, is no easy task. We experience the incredible beauty of being a parent because He does. And we also experience the great, great love that makes us want the very best for our baby—even when the very best is not happening.

But here's where His design comes with a release valve. According to the Bible, the Holy Spirit is our Comforter (Jeremiah 8:18

NIV). Although pain is inevitable in the love of a parent, the comfort of God is just as inevitable. His promise is strong. He will carry you in times of sorrow. His wisdom will guide you through the hardest times. His own love for you will shelter and surround you as you weep or grieve. It will hurt. It will be hard. But with His comfort, you'll come out stronger than before.

Nothing truly prepares us as parents. That includes all the incredible happy times as well as all the difficult times. There's so much that only time and experience can shed light on. But the Bible is full of promises for *all* times and situations. When you need God most, He will be there. You can turn to His promises for all seasons. And when you need it, His comfort will get you through.

 PRAYER

*Father, I understand that pain is a part
of the parenting process. Prepare my heart
so that I won't be alarmed when it comes.
I will also choose not to be helpless.
I will trust Your comfort.
Please come quickly, Lord;
shelter me and show me the way through.*

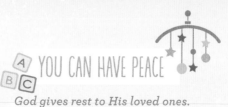

YOU CAN HAVE PEACE

God gives rest to His loved ones.
PSALM 127:2 NLT

This one goes out to the tired. The sleepless. The mama on a one-and-a-half-hour feeding schedule. The dad who wonders whether he'll ever feel ready for these twins. The ones who see the midnight and early-morning hours now more than they did when they pulled all-nighters in college. You may feel lonely in the dark...but you are not alone.

It's a fair assumption that God pulled some all-nighters while creating the world, don't you think? And at the end of that week, after weaving the manes of lions, causing water to fall over rocky cliffs, breathing language into whales, and—finally—intricately carving Adam and Eve into life, God rested (Genesis 2:3).

The Hebrew word for *rest* in the Creation story outlined in Genesis is *shabath*, which literally means "to stop." When we think of rest, we tend to think in terms of relaxation: catching up on a favorite show, catching a nap, reading a good book, or scrolling through social media. But simply put, resting means ceasing. No worrying. No trying. Just trusting.

Being still. Knowing that God is in control.

Sleep is a hot commodity for new parents. We can't manage the amount of sleep we get—our newborns often take on the role of management at that stage. It can feel pretty helpless. There are certain things we can do, like choosing a nap over doing the dishes when baby finally sleeps during the day. But no matter how hard we try, for a time our sleep patterns will be off and we will be exhausted.

Rest, however, is a waking activity. This we can do: we can *shabath*. While feeding baby, we can close our eyes and focus on things that are true, right, lovely, noble, and pure (Philippians 4:8). We can give worries to God. We can do the simple act of stopping, sitting, letting our minds wander, and enjoying the moment. What do you think God was doing after creating the world? Probably admiring its incredible beauty. You can do the same. Sleep may be for later. But resting is for now.

 PRAYER

Father, teach me to shabath the way
You meant it to be. Thank You for this season
where I can rely more heavily on
Your shabath rest and enjoy the beauty of
Your creation, my sweet baby.

YOUR FATHER LOVES YOU

The LORD your God is with you....
He will take great delight in you...
He will ... rejoice over you with singing.
ZEPHANIAH 3:17 NIV

It's been a long day. Not a bad one, to be sure but with all the busyness and to-dos, relationships to maintain, feedings and burpings, tiredness, issues to deal with and new things to celebrate ... the day has just gotten away from you. And now, for the first time, you are coming into a quiet moment. The baby is in your arms. The diaper is clean and the swaddle is ready to do its work. You rock gently, staring again at those peaceful lips, the closed eyes, the fine hair, the tiny fingernails. You feel the weight of your baby, however light. You hear soft breathing and occasional coos. It's easier, at this moment, to believe that all is right in the world. It's easier to remind yourself that God is in charge. That the story has an ending and the ending is good! Snuggling this little miracle, it seems like the most natural thing in the world to sway back and forth, humming softly over the baby.

Perhaps it seems so natural because it's exactly how your Father in heaven treats you. He has such tenderness for you. No matter how jaded a person becomes, in God's eyes we are still His sweet babies. Not that everything we do delights Him. But He sees us as a mother sees her toddler: unwise to the world's ways, vulnerable in emotion, and doing our best with what we've been given. A mother wouldn't berate her toddler for falling down while learning to run any more than God would punish us for doing our best and falling short.

In the quiet of the night, when you can turn off the worries and the busyness, a still, small voice comes through. It's the voice of love. It's the one that softly hums, gently rocks your spirit against His chest, and quietly whispers that He's proud of who you are and all that you are becoming. Every time you snuggle your little one ... remember that Someone is snuggling you too.

 PRAYER

Father, Your arms are a refuge and
Your voice is like home base.
Tuck me in each night with the same care
and love that I feel as I tuck in
my little one.

GOD'S GUIDANCE IS FOR YOU

All your children will be taught by the LORD,
and great will be their peace.
ISAIAH 54:13 NIV

Making decisions for our children apart from God's guidance is a little like playing Candyland. Who knows what color we'll get when we flip over that card—it could send us four squares forward or two squares back. But when we rely on God's promises to walk behind us and gently guide us to the right or the left, it brings confidence and the hope for amazing things to happen.

When baby penguins are born, their ears are calibrated to the unique frequency created by the sound of their parents' voices. This isn't just a handy thing for living in the penguin neighborhood, because to the human eye all penguins look alike! Penguin parents must leave their chicks, along with all the other chicks, to go hunt for food. Imagine the chaos when all the penguin parents come back to the newly born chicks, searching for their little guy in the huddle! Imagine the hubbub when hundreds of nearly identical black-and-white squawkers start hollering for their baby Henry. "Hey! Over here! No, over here!

No, not that one! Wait, are you Henry? No? Have you seen him? He's gray and little, with soft feathers..." That's why each penguin parent has its own unique vocal frequency. And why the baby learns it quickly.

When penguin parents return to their young, they only need to call out. And in the midst of all the other families, the parents and babies find each other.

As humans, we each have our own unique DNA. And amazingly, we come prewired to know our heavenly Father's voice. It may look and sound different to us than to anyone else on the planet. But the imprint God gives us is recognizable to us—that's a promise.

As parents, the best thing we can do is to pray for our children to listen for that voice. We can train them to recognize the sound and feel of their heavenly Father in their lives. And we can look forward to the peace that will reign in them as they grow closer to the One who created them.

PRAYER

God, it is so important that my child know You. Thank You for Your promise to love, care for, and teach my baby. Amen.

YOU NEED A VILLAGE

Live in harmony with one another.
ROMANS 12:16 NIV

The African buffalo has a unique practice of voting, as in a democracy. Only adult females participate. But when the herd is deciding which way to travel, individual females will stand up, look in a certain direction, then lie back down. Majority wins.

Elephants are known to be socially complex. They live in families, and adults cooperate to provide food, childcare, defense, and decision-making.

Female mule deer have a pact with other adult females in the group. When one goes out hunting, she leaves her babies near another mama deer. If a predator comes, the babysitter mama will protect her own babies as well as the babies of the hunting mom.

Many other animal species seem to have an innate understanding of the importance of community. And it's no different for humans. God designed us to work together, to love one another, to care for one another, and to live close. There are fifty-nine "one another" commands in the New Testament. Some of the commands include:

- Be at peace with each other (Mark 9:50).
- Wash one another's feet (John 13:14).

- Love one another (John 13:34).
- Be devoted to one another in brotherly love (Romans 12:10).
- Honor one another above yourselves (Romans 12:10).

Think God was serious about making sure that we know we belong together? And that we be together with respect and love for one another?

A new parent will most likely feel alone at some point, since a newborn takes so much energy and time. But as soon as you can, reach out to those around you. Hopefully you'll have some folks reach out to you too. But don't fret if they don't. Since we're designed for community, we can pray and ask God to bring that community our way. That might mean taking some risks on our part. But we can trust Him when He calls us into something. Inviting others into our lives has the potential to make life infinitely richer. It's a priceless gift to watch other adults love our children. And it's a priceless gift to share the gift of life with one another.

PRAYER

God, thank You for the people in my life who love and support me. Bring healthy, strong individuals into the life of my baby. And help me to pour into others' lives as well.

YOU'LL GET THERE

Press on toward the goal.
PHILIPPIANS 3:14 NIV

Being a new parent is unlike any other time in a person's life. It's full of amazing new feelings and experiences. It can also be extremely hard in some ways.

Even if there were a rule book for parenting, there would be so many "exception to the rule" scenarios because every single child, parent, and family is different. The best thing we can do is get up each morning with a prayer and a good sense of humor.

Cliff Young was a sixty-one-year-old potato farmer who entered the Sydney ultramarathon in 1983. He'd spent his life chasing after sheep, sometimes running two or three days to catch them all. So, he said, five days wouldn't be that different. That's the amount of time expected for this 544-mile race. At the end of the first day, Mr. Young was so far behind that he had no idea the other runners had stopped to sleep for six hours, or that it was expected he do so. He carried on. For five days. He ran without stopping. And he ended up beating the other competitors by ten hours. His approach of nonstop jogging put him two days ahead of the previously held ultramarathon record in Australia.

Like Mr. Young, you are embarking on a journey you've only trained for by living your life. You've shown up in your street clothes (Mr. Young was wearing overalls for the ultramarathon) and can only imagine what lies in store for you. But like Mr. Young, you don't need to run fast. Just keep putting one foot in front of the other. Wash the dishes, again. Feed and burp and change, again. Teach, play, discipline, and hug. Help with homework. Drive to practices. Referee siblings. Agonize and dream and pray and love. Always love.

Parenthood is full of rewardless moments. But the prize comes at the end when God acknowledges you and blesses you for loving His kids so well.

 PRAYER

Lord, I trust You to give me all
I need each day as I parent. I trust that
You've been training me for this season.
I will do my best, putting one foot in front of
the other and enjoying the journey as I go.

YOU'RE SURROUNDED BY GOOD

Taste and see that the LORD is good.
PSALM 34:8 CSB

Goodness is everywhere—all the time, in all the places, especially when we're looking for it. God's goodness is in all the snuggles of a newborn, the siblings and cousins growing up together, the first birthday parties and special playtimes. There is good.

Goodness is in the slow cooker in fall, with its sliced vegetables and sizzling meat, delicious spices, and the promise of a warm meal on a chilly evening. In a world that holds tables to gather around, family to break bread with, and meals to be made, there is still good.

God's goodness is in the laundry pile, with its whites and bright colors and the *swish-swash* of the washer. There's goodness in the *whoosh* of the vacuum as it cleans up dog hair and crumbs from games played and snacks enjoyed. There's goodness in picking up tiny toys and stacking books on shelves and going to the store for shampoo and bananas. There's goodness in checking in with family via texts, keeping the calendars up-to-date, and placing books on hold at the library.

God, who loves us as much as He did on

day one, makes all things work for the good of those who love Him. He thinks of us constantly, more than there are grains of sand. He created the heat of summer, the colors of autumn, the glittering snow of winter, and the newness of life in spring. He went to the grave and back for me and for you. In a world overflowing with reminders of God's love, there is still good. Walking to school. A thought-provoking sermon at church. Fresh-fallen snow. The width and depth of the ocean and the warmth of the sun. The crisp pages of a new, blank journal. A hot latte. A letter from a friend. Daisies growing out of a sidewalk crack. Your children, friends, and family. A verse in Scripture that speaks straight to the heart. Goodness isn't hard to find, especially when you're on the lookout. May you see the goodness of the Lord, right there in your every day (which is really anything but ordinary).

 PRAYER

God, help me to truly find joy
in the ordinary of my days.
Thank You for giving me a family,
a baby, a home, and a life worth
finding all the good in.

The name of the LORD is a strong tower;
the righteous run to it and are safe.
PROVERBS 18:10 NKJV

Though you've slept for hours, you feel as if your head just hit the pillow. Already, your mind is swirling with thoughts for the day. Of course there's the usual getting ready, making coffee, facing traffic ... But there's more weighing on your mind than the daily grind. That conversation you had with your spouse the other night just didn't sit right, and you're worried you're drifting apart. Your baby only says three words and the milestone says it should be ten. There's a boss to please and laundry to fold, bills to pay and church to attend. You start to feel as if you should hide somewhere and hope everything works out.

Sometimes escape seems like the most logical conclusion when we're faced with the overwhelming circumstances of life. After all, modern psychology tells us that we are programmed for either fight or flight when perceived trouble rolls around. Right? The question is: without adequate strength to fight, will you run to the only refuge on this earth with power great enough to protect you and keep you safe forever?

God says His name is a strong tower and the righteous run to it and find safety. He assures us that no one who comes to Him for protection will be turned away. He is our fortress, our secret place where we can hide, and He Himself will fight the big and small battles we face each day. There is no better place to go than to the only One with the power to save you in this moment and in your lifetime.

There's a lot to balance with all the hats we wear. God doesn't want us to tuck Him into a corner and visit Him when it's convenient. Instead, He wants to be the flavor of every moment of your day. God wants you to be encouraged in every portion of your life. So hang out in that tower called His Name. It will be safe, warm, and comforting in everything you do.

PRAYER

In everything today, Lord Jesus.
In all I do. In all I say. In all I experience.
In everyone I meet. In the name of Jesus.

YOU ARE LOVED

No power in the sky above
or in the earth below—
indeed, nothing in all creation
will ever be able to separate us
from the love of God that is revealed
in Christ Jesus our Lord.
ROMANS 8:39 NLT

The "twos" are only "terrible" if you think of them that way—which is sometimes *very* easy to do. But, really, age two is a lot like us, to God. Twos have big feelings. Twos want their way. Twos stomp their feet and cry if you cut the crust off their sandwich even though they asked for that five minutes prior. Twos sometimes have accidents. Twos often make messes. But they're learning, growing, and desperately need your love and guidance.

No matter how well we do or do not measure up, God just keeps on loving us the way He does. He actually enjoys us. He knocks on the door of our lives, and in some weird way He actually delights in us. Here we are—people who routinely break His heart. We surely frustrate Him. We think we are little gods running the show. We misbehave. But He keeps on knocking on the door, keeps on loving us. That's the one thing we all have to know.

The most liberating truth in all the universe is this: Jesus is absurdly and ravenously in love with us. He is for us. He is for you! You might turn your back on Him, change your mind about Him, stomp your feet at Him, or run away from Him. But He will never, ever leave your side. You might fall, stumble, trip, fumble, sin, grumble, and make a general mess of things. But He can't not love you. He made a way back, a way up, a way out, and a way in. He came for you, all the way to earth, to rescue you. And He's not giving up on you now. Let God drop that truth into your heart. Hear Him tell you how He loves you with a reckless love. And nothing, absolutely nothing, can stand in the way of it.

PRAYER

*Father, thank You for loving me
no matter what. Through Your example,
help me to love my child through the ups
and downs of all the years.*

HE TAKES YOUR BURDENS

He has shown you, O man, what is good;
and what does the LORD require of you
but to do justly, to love mercy,
and to walk humbly with your God?
MICAH 6:8 NKJV

When you're a parent, you are quickly reminded that almost any job or activity can take up the entire amount of time you give it. In other words, margin is not created by accident. We need to actually look for, and sometimes fight for, that extra space in our days and lives to breathe. Which is very difficult to do, as we turn so much of our focus to raising our children well.

There will always be new joys to discover, milestones to reach, problems to solve, or standards we want so hard to meet. While this means limitless possibilities, it also means that life will not be the one knocking on our door and asking us whether we have the necessary built-in margin. What if we looked at margin as something we must schedule, prioritize, and treat seriously? Sometimes we worry that if we do make way for this intentional time of solitude, stillness, or room to "just be," we will compromise our other areas of attention. But what would happen if we demanded margin? What would it feel like to set some time for yourself every day to rest in the arms of your loving Father? And maybe the better question is: what could happen if you don't? Is it possible that if we do not demand margin from ourselves, the other areas of our life will naturally suffer?

By allowing ourselves to have true free time, our heart remembers what we naturally enjoy. We are far more inclined to take a walk around the neighborhood, read an inspiring book, or get back to our green thumb. Our passion is reignited and we give ourselves space to think, to receive instruction from God, to learn more about our gifts, and to remember the purpose behind this whole thing called life.

Margin multiplies itself—always. Any time we spend with God doing whatever it is we love to do is never wasted. We become more efficient employees, more compassionate friends, more patient parents, more respectful romantic partners, and more intentional, aware people.

 PRAYER

Jesus, thank You for creating the gift of time and for guiding us in how to spend that time. Show us how to create margin in life and teach us how to be still with You. Thank You for multiplying the time we give You and guiding us down paths of diligence.

YOUR WORDS MAKE A DIFFERENCE

Encourage one another.
I THESSALONIANS 5:11 NIV

f you've ever done a 5K (a 3.1-mile walk or run) in your community, you've probably found it pretty encouraging. Depending on the race and the reason for it, you'll find yourself in crowds of energized people on a common mission: get to the finish line. For fun. They may be dressed in colorful costumes or tutus. They may be in groups or wearing shirts supporting friends with breast cancer. They may be pushing strollers. They may be dressed in their military uniforms and carrying flags. And most likely if you say "Good job" to them, they'll smile and say "You too!" with enthusiasm.

In a 5K, some people are in it to win and some are in it to finish with a smile. Almost everyone has a story behind their jog. Some people run one in their lifetime and call it quits, while others collect finisher medals like they're candy. But the common ground is showing up, usually early in the morning on a Saturday, and following the same path to the finish line.

As a new parent, it's so important to have

others on the journey with you. Most likely it's a spouse, sharing the same short nights and the same long days. You will both be worn out from running. But you're also both in it for the same reason: to cross the finish line strong, hopefully with smiles on your faces. You can lean on one another as you go. Cheer each other on! Remind each other of the good job you're doing—and that when it gets tough, you can still put one foot in front of the other. Remind one another to hydrate and rest. Maybe wear a sparkly tutu from time to time, just to keep the mood light. As new parents, a sense of humor goes a very long way!

As a new parent, you'll definitely need encouragement. But you'll also benefit from lifting up your spouse emotionally, as well as anyone else who crosses your path. We were made to encourage—and, strangely, encouraging others will fill us up too.

 PRAYER

Father, even in my tiredness or stress,
help me to see ways that I can show kindness
to those around me. And bring people
into my life who will use their words
to give me strength, as well.

YOU CAN HAVE GOD'S WILL

Your kingdom come. Your will be done
on earth as it is in heaven.
LUKE 11:2 NKJV

Not sure how to pray? What to say? What to expect, hope for, ask, or want? Oftentimes we know what we *don't* want. We also want to see a situation resolve in the way God would choose. So, how do we line ourselves up with His heart?

There's no clear definition in the Bible of God's will. We often pray, "if it's Your will," but without an understanding of what that means, isn't it a little bit of a guess? Perhaps the closest thing to a definition of God's will comes in what we call the Lord's Prayer (found in Matthew chapter 6 and Luke chapter 11): "Your will be done on earth as it is in heaven." *On earth as it is in heaven.* We are instructed to pray that the way God operates His kingdom in heaven is what we should pray for here on earth.

Is there sickness in heaven? Pray against sickness on earth. Are there broken relationships in heaven? Pray for relationships to heal on earth. A mother learns during labor that the umbilical cord is wrapped around the baby's neck and the baby is in danger. There is no physical harm in heaven, so she prays for the baby's safety. A new mom experiences postpartum depression. There is no depression in heaven—after all, the source of all hope—Jesus—is there! So her husband prays with her for depression to leave. There's a very long list of reasons why we pray, especially as new parents. But if we're wondering how to pray for our children or our current situation, we need only to look as far as God's kingdom. The Bible helps us understand how God operates—and that is a very good guideline for how to pray.

Jesus is always the best example for how to operate. He was in touch with His Father, so His prayers were always answered. As you embark on your parenthood journey, be encouraged by the way Jesus operated and know that you can pray for the very best for your family. For your home. Right here, as it is in heaven.

PRAYER

Father, I want Your will in all things. Please guide me in how to pray for the things You want for me, my baby, and my family.

IN EVERYTHING
TODAY, LORD...
JESUS.
IN ALL I DO.
IN ALL I SAY.
IN ALL I
EXPERIENCE.
IN HIS NAME.

ONE THING YOU MUST KNOW

I focus on this one thing...
looking forward to what lies ahead,
I press on to reach the end of the race.
PHILIPPIANS 3:13–14 NLT

When you first become pregnant, somewhere deep inside, you may begin with an attitude of "getting past this." You know the hormones will surge, but then they'll settle. You expect to feel tired, but then the baby will start sleeping more and it will be okay. You just need to get your groove back. Get your schedule figured out. Get back to work, back to social activities, back to life. Having a baby changes everything, sure. But then everything will settle down and it will be much like it was before kids, right? *Right?*

But until you experience the new normal, you don't truly understand what that means. It means *everything*, at least on the daily, is different. And it will never, ever go back to being the way it was. This might sound scary or sad ... and yes, there may be some grieving when it comes to remembering the extra time or sleep or focus you once had. But the sooner your heart reconciles with the changes, the sooner you will settle into the peace that passes understanding.

If you spent your entire young life living on the coast, at sea level, you would be used to a certain fitness level. Maybe you're even a triathlon athlete. Then you move to Denver, which has an altitude of over five thousand feet. You learn very quickly that your body needs to adjust to the new altitude. You feel for a while like you are no longer an athlete. You pant when you jog. You tire quickly. But over time, your body adjusts to the new normal—and it actually makes you a stronger competitor when you travel back to your hometown on the coast!

Your new normal, as a parent, is like Denver. You're gasping for air, missing the ocean. You'll get glimpses of the past when you visit there, but it will never be the same. Your high-altitude home has caused you to change the way you live. But in the end, it will make you stronger and bring so much joy.

 PRAYER

God, I trust You in this new place.
Strengthen my body for what's ahead,
and help me look back on the past
with happiness and gratitude.

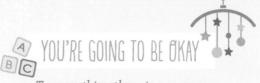

YOU'RE GOING TO BE OKAY

To everything there is a season,
a time for every purpose under heaven.
ECCLESIASTES 3:1 NKJV

There are a few things about seasons that are worth noting:

Seasons *change*. Depending on where you live, *how* they change may vary. But regardless, time is marked by a cycle of seasons that is inevitable.

Seasons *feel different*. In winter in the northern hemisphere, winter temperatures top out at a cooler number than in summer. Leaves on deciduous trees change colors, fall to the ground, stay dormant, and pop out in spring. Humidity marks the warmer temps in Southern summers. Sheep, deer, cows, and other animals have their babies in the spring. Thanksgiving gives the fall a warm and cozy sense.

Seasons *overlap*. Although they have calendar dates to mark them, it's not as if on March 21 every tulip blooms and every lamb is born. We might have snow in spring, and we might have hot weather in early fall. Dates just give us guidelines—a sense that a new season is coming.

Life is a lot like the changing of seasons. And nothing makes that clearer than having a baby. Time is marked by milestones that fluctuate from baby to baby. When will they sleep through the night? When will they cut a tooth? When will they sit up, crawl, walk, or say their first word? And most importantly, will they do it "on time"? We rely on literature and experts to tell us whether our baby is up to speed. We waste time worrying about development instead of enjoying the moment we're in right then.

How often do we hear someone talking about sand and sea when it's 30 degrees and snowing? Or wishing for snow when the air conditioner breaks down? Instead of pining away for greener grass, what would it look like if you focused on thankfulness for the season you're in? Your baby will hit milestones. You will get through every challenge. There will be smiles, laughter, tummy tickles, tears, tantrums, accidents, and special sweet moments every step of the way. Your sweet baby will say "Mama." And she will eventually get a fever, also. Your baby will need you, love you, and amaze you. Soak up the season you're in and look forward to whatever is next.

 PRAYER

Lord, thank You for my sweet baby and all of the many seasons we will go through together. I will anticipate the good and trust You through it all.

YOU WON'T FAIL

God is within her;
she will not be toppled.
PSALM 46:5 CSB

Having a baby means blazing new trails for your life. And if you've ever watched a jungle-adventure movie, you know that blazing trails can be scary! In the jungle, monkeys and snakes could fall from the trees and attack. Tigers or gorillas find you in their territory and you're a goner. Poisonous plants and spiders are just waiting for you to get close. And never mind if you wander near the camp of a native warrior...

Okay, having a baby isn't *that* scary! But sometimes as new parents, it feels as if we're ill-equipped to handle this new territory. Our angry monkeys might look like all the details of a house that just won't stay clean by itself. Our constricting snakes might be the time and attention that a baby requires when the rest of life hasn't really slowed down. Our vicious tigers could be fears and worries that sneak mercilessly into our thoughts at all hours but especially in the dark of night during our fleeting chances for sleep. And our poisonous plants could be the social media we consume, watching others' highlight reels and wondering if we really are cut out for this baby thing at all.

But this is a promise: God is on your side. As our fortress, we have Him to rest in, hide behind, and call on. Trekking through the jungle of parenthood, God is the shade that protects us from falling snakes or monkeys. When we stay under Him, we learn to accept what details we can affect today and let the rest go. God is our armor. When constricting time wants to squeeze in, His schedule allows us to breathe and relax. God is our camouflage, allowing us to pass unscathed through worries and fears as we hand them to Him time and time again. And God's Word is mind-renewing water that refreshes us and helps us keep a right perspective on the world.

Leaning on God as we go, we can't fail as parents. We will fall. We will make mistakes. But we will get up again, and more likely than not the good will far outweigh the hard.

 PRAYER

Father, with You as my guard I'll thrive
as a parent. Thank You for Your promises.
I receive all the help You offer.

YOUR BABY IS UNIQUE

I knew you before I formed you
in your mother's womb.
JEREMIAH 1:5 NLT

Minutes after your little one is born, a nurse brings in an ink pad and a document. She pats your baby's foot on the pad, then gently touches it to the paper. Later she hands you the prints of your baby's feet, and you marvel at them ... their tiny size, perfect shape, and intricate creases. This is *your* baby. The little thing that has grown with you for nine months now has footprints. And you're in awe.

In a year's time, you start seeing those same smudgy prints on kitchen floors, with matching handprints on windows and water cups. Slightly annoying, but also pretty cute. These are *your* baby's marks, just like everyone else's and yet totally unique. Someone could lift those prints from their surfaces and match them to your child and yours alone.

Those prints—so special and detailed that not even an artist could recreate them—were hand-tooled by their Creator.

"You saw me before I was born. Every day of my life was recorded in Your book. Every moment was laid out before a single day had passed" (Psalm 139:16 NLT).

"Even before He made the world, God loved us and chose us in Christ to be holy and without fault in His eyes" (Ephesians 1:4 NLT).

"You watched me as I was being formed in utter seclusion, as I was woven together in the dark of the womb. You saw me before I was born...." (Psalm 139:15–16 NLT).

Footprints and fingerprints are daily reminders that God knows every single detail about us. He made the blueprints, designed the dream of us, and then molded us into the perfect little human form that emerges into the world. And with that kind of care, we can let our baby's prints remind us of many things. We can remember that God cares even more than we do about our baby's future. We can remember that He has a wonderful plan for our baby and for each of us as parents and people. And we can remember that His indelible print is left on each of us, made in His image, and capable of more than we can even imagine.

PRAYER

Lord, Your hand creates beautiful work,
and I know my baby is beautiful.
Help us to fulfill the calling that
You've designed us for.

YOUR LOVE WILL GROW

That you, being rooted and grounded
in love, may be able to comprehend
with all the saints what is the width
and length and depth and height—to know
the love of Christ which passes knowledge.
EPHESIANS 3:17–19 NKJV

One of the great myths of new parenthood is that if you don't fall immediately, irreversibly, wholeheartedly in love with your baby the moment you lay eyes on that sweet little bundle, there's something wrong with your "parenter." And you *may* do just that: you might experience that once-in-a-lifetime heartburst like a thousand fizzy Pop Rocks exploding inside you, unleashing a love that you never knew was possible. If you do, consider yourself one of the very, very blessed ones.

If you don't, though—if your emotions come on gradually or even if you struggle to feel connected to your baby—please know that it's going to be okay.

Every single parent has one thing in common from the first days forward: *growth*. Imagine three different couples. Couple A falls instantly in love when their eyes meet across a crowded room. Couple B goes through college together as friends, and then one day they finally realize their friendship has become more than that. Couple C meets on a dating app. They both get the sense that God has brought them together to be married. All three couples get engaged and then tie the knot.

One, two, five, ten years later, each of these couples, no matter their start, have grown *tons*. They've learned so much. They've had major ups and downs. But the love they have is deeper and wiser than ever. Each of them, no matter their start, goes through the up-and-down journey of marriage.

When you met your little one, was it love at first sight? Or was it different? It can be hard, not feeling an instant connection. But it does not mean you're broken. Be patient. Just like the instant heartburst parents, you have years and years of growing to do. Your love for your baby will come on strong. That's a promise. Trust the Lord and His perfect design for you and your family.

PRAYER

God, I want to love my baby in the most authentic, effective, beautiful way possible. Pour out Your love on me so that I can lavish it on this child.

YOU AND YOUR SPOUSE ARE A TEAM

A cord of three strands is not easily broken.
ECCLESIASTES 4:12 CSB

There is a survey you can take that measures the impact of major life events over the course of twelve months. It lists forty-three events, beginning with the death of a spouse (scoring 100) and ending with a traffic ticket (scoring 11). Between those two is a rainbow of reasons we may be stressed. The idea is to add up each event you've experienced in the past year to see how stress may be impacting your health. "Pregnancy" is listed as #12. "Gaining a new family member" is #14. Combined, these two events add up to 79 points on the scale out of 100!

What's the point, you ask? Having a baby is a major stressor! You and your spouse will need each other more than ever. Together you'll figure out the diaper thing, the feeding thing, the bathing thing, and all the other things that come with having an irresistibly snuggly new creature in your home.

Disagreements with your spouse *will* happen. There's so much new and unknown. You've had different upbringings and experiences. And as much as you might discuss parenting philosophies pre-newborn, putting them into practice is a whole new ordeal.

In the 2020 NFL season, Tom Brady played for the Tampa Bay Buccaneers after twenty seasons with the New England Patriots. As a Patriot, Brady had won six Super Bowls and multiple MVP awards. So hopes were high for the Buccaneers at the start of 2020. But the first game of the season did not go well. It wasn't that Brady had become a bad player overnight. But he was on a new team, running plays he'd never run with teammates he'd never been in a game with before. It would take time, effort, and learning for him to connect well with a whole new team.

You and your spouse are running plays you've never run before. No matter how incredible your problem-solving, communication, and relationship skills are, they will be shaken with a new baby. But in the end, you can be confident that you are meant to be a team and that, with practice, you'll get the win.

 PRAYER

Marriage is hard, Lord, and parenting adds to the equation. Now more than ever we need You. Grow us closer together. Let this little one strengthen our family in every way.

YOUR OTHER KIDS WILL MAKE IT TOO

Two are better than one because
they have a good reward for their efforts.
ECCLESIASTES 4:9 CSB

f this is your first baby, then you might not be thinking about other children in the family just yet. Maybe tuck away this devotion for a year or three and come back to it when it's relevant. But if you do have another one at home, then you know. There is considerable anxiety and wonder to be had regarding how older children will handle having a new baby in the house.

Some toddlers handle the transition better than others. Some *parents* do too, for that matter. But you simply can't get around the fact that bringing home a baby changes everything for your older child. Your oldest has always had your undivided attention. They've been the baby. You've been their playmate, provider, and protector. And now they have to share all those precious spoils with someone else. That's not an easy thing!

Your older child might get downright mean for a while. They might take on a new behavior such as kicking, hitting, biting, or throwing food. If they were potty trained, even that might go away. You may find that your older child gets quieter and shy or do the complete opposite by demonstrating anger toward the new baby. One of the harder things for parents is that we have no idea how our other children will react. We have to take it as it comes.

But if you ever feel overwhelmed by it all, remember this—millions and billions of families have gone before you. Once your older child finds their groove, realizes that your love for them actually grows instead of shrinks, finds all of their needs met, and—most likely—starts enjoying having a sibling to play with, you'll see the good in it all. Nobody *likes* to share, of course—but everyone knows it's a good practice. So you're giving your toddler (and your baby, as he or she grows) necessary life skills. And the love between siblings is truly one of a kind. That dynamic will bless your heart and home for years to come.

PRAYER

*Father, You have chosen to make this
a multi-child household, so we know
it's right for our family. Comfort our older
child while the new one comes in.
Give our older one all the assurance needed
to feel safe and secure with us.*

YOUR HELP WILL COME

I look up to the mountains—
does my help come from there?
My help comes from the LORD,
who made heaven and earth!
PSALM 121:1-2 NLT

Maybe you fall into the category of new parents who have people really wanting to reach out to you. You're getting meal train calls, offers to host baby showers, new grands wanting to come hold the baby so you can sleep after the birth, and more. Or you may be in the category of people who don't live near family or help. It might be a lonely time and hard to think of how you're going to do all of this alone. I'd love to receive help, you say, if only there were help being offered.

There is a message for each of you, and although it may look like different messages for each, the heart of it is the same. New parenthood is hard. Emotions tug, babies cry, bodies need to heal. *Receive*, knowing that God has you covered.

We were designed for the good works that God set out for us to do. It might be more comfortable to be the one doing the kind things most of the time. But in order for us to fulfill our good works, there must be recipients. And new parents are almost exclusively recipients for a while. Others are truly blessed when they get to serve another. After all, they're not on the payroll here. They are offering because they love you. And love *serves*.

You might not have people knocking down your door during this new baby time. Loneliness is definitely painful, and baby-ing is definitely hard, but God promises to never forsake our needs. He will provide for you. You *will* sleep, you *will* eat, you *will* get to share the sweet excitement of your new baby with those who love you. It just might not look like what you expect. You have the special opportunity to see this time as a season where the Lord is tucking you under His wing to nurse you into a new place in His heart.

In all cases, receiving help at this time may come from friends or in less conventional ways. But it all comes from God's heart, straight to you and your sweet little one.

૯ ૯ ૯ PRAYER

God, I receive Your love, in all its forms, in any way You choose to deliver. Amen.

FEELINGS ARE YOUR HELPERS

From the end of the earth I will cry to You,
when my heart is overwhelmed;
lead me to the rock that is higher than I.
PSALM 61:2 NKJV

"It's okay to *want* to shake your baby. It's not okay to actually shake your baby." Her words were wise for the new mama. An outsider might hear that statement and think it didn't need to be said—after all, who doesn't know that it's not okay to hurt a child?

But as a new parent, you're at one of your most vulnerable times of life. Your defenses are down because your love is at a whole new level. You aren't sleeping. Your routines are out the window. You're not used to the sounds of a baby's most natural form of communication—crying. Sometimes constant crying. There's nothing you want more than to comfort your baby and give him what he needs. So a crying baby can lead to feelings of such helplessness. Emotions get raw.

Like the speedometer and the gas gauge in a car, feelings tell us when it's time to do something different. You drive until the gas light comes on, and you know that if you don't act fast, you'll be stuck on the side of the road.

You watch the numbers on the speedometer, knowing that if they exceed the sign you just passed, you may see flashing lights in your rearview mirror. So you slow down. Feelings are similar. You can be exceedingly happy, indicating that this is a moment to savor. You can be super sad, indicating that you need to have a good cry or talk to someone. If you're angry and overwhelmed, it might just be time to step away for a minute and take a few deep breaths.

Absolutely no one can blame you for feeling a certain way. It's what you do about it in the moment that makes the difference. Adopt one or two plans for those moments when you need to take a breather. And always remember that God is just a breath away, waiting to comfort you. Truly.

 PRAYER

Father, in the moments when I feel
out of control, wrap me in Your arms
and remind me that it's going to be okay.
Keep my baby safe and surround
our family with Your love.

EVERY DAY WILL BLESS YOU

Teach us to number our days,
that we may gain a heart of wisdom.
PSALM 90:12 NIV

Chances are, you've experienced some version of the post-Thanksgiving meal blahs. You know, those sounds of *oof* and *uggh* emerging from the living room as overfed family members lean back in comfy chairs. We rub our bellies through outstretched yoga pants, not regretting all that delicious food. Well, maybe we do a little. But not enough to leave that pumpkin pie all lonely on the kitchen counter.... Mostly we just wonder how in the world we went from happy and excited to overstuffed and drowsy in the matter of thirty minutes.

Chances are, you've also heard the phrase "It all goes so fast" in relation to how quickly children grow up. As trite as it sounds, once you have your little one, you understand. It can be so very easy to want the hectic days to settle down. You want the potty-training days to be in your rearview mirror. You pine away for the times before mac and cheese were the plate du jour again. And again. And again.

God knows that parenting littles is hard. So

He has this beautiful way of weaving gems into the tapestry of our ordinary. These gems might come the first time your toddler says "I wub woo, Mama!" They might sparkle every time your sweet one falls asleep on your chest. They come in hugs and snuggles, adorable shoes, and even cuter toes that fit in them. They appear in happy, splashy bath times and spontaneous pre-bedtime dance parties. These gems might be easy to pass up. But they are the little gifts deposited throughout our days that are made to be cherished.

It will go slow. And it will go fast. But only you can reach in to pull out every drop of savoring you can find. Just like appreciating every smooth bite of Aunt Sarah's stuffing and Grandpa George's succulent turkey— the more you love every moment, the more wonderful memories you'll have to look back on as your little one grows.

 PRAYER

Help me catch every sweet moment You throw at me, Lord. Help me to cherish my baby amid the everyday moments.
I don't want to miss a thing.

CHOOSE YOUR MARRIAGE

As the Scriptures say, "A man leaves his father and mother to get married, and he becomes like one person with his wife."
EPHESIANS 5:31 CEV

In the first days of a newborn's life, everything centers around your baby. Yes, your new bundle of joy has successfully turned your world upside down—and you're generally okay with that. Days previously fraught with activity are now slow and deliberate, with lots of time to snuggle and stare. And at the center of it all is a tiny seven-pound wonder, sleeping, eating, and generally drawing every single eye and heart his or her way.

After a while, the very-newness settles down. Mama and Daddy slowly bring bits of other life back in. One or both might go back to work. Meal trains eventually chug to a halt and cooking becomes part of the routine again. And where all eyes were once on Baby, slowly they shift back toward their surroundings of home, life, and marriage.

When the new-baby dust settles, God's design for families hasn't changed: He always comes first. And second is our spouse. We all know that if we have a healthy, connected marriage, our kids will grow up blessed. The addition of a new family member—one who will *very* soon start observing, mirroring, and learning from every move you make—makes connecting as a couple a priority. But between the feedings and the bathings and the dishes and the dirty diapers and the burpings and the....well, you fill in the blanks ... how can you possibly concentrate on your spouse?

The truth is, God wants you to thrive as a couple. He knows how hard it is. He loves you, your spouse, and your child so much. So the more you lean on Him, as an individual and as a couple, the more you'll see His ability to bring you even closer together.

In the midst of all the new, what would it look like to keep your relationship with your spouse top of mind? Maybe start thanking God for your spouse every time you notice them helping you or your baby. Ask God to be at work in your marriage during this crazy season. Kiss often. Hold hands. Talk to each other about the good things God is doing. Your baby will be all the better for it. And you will too.

PRAYER

Father, I want my marriage to be strong—
for my sake, for the sake of my child,
and for Your glory. Show my spouse and me
what it looks like to prioritize You
and then us in this special season.

YOU DO YOU

I will send you the Helper from the Father;
He is the Spirit of truth who comes
from the Father.
JOHN 15:26 NCV

There's something about becoming a new parent that puts a flashing neon sign on your forehead signaling, *"now accepting unsolicited advice."* As if it weren't enough to be bombarded on social media with input of every sort imaginable. You now have your own veritable smorgasbord of parents and in-laws, siblings, friends, and perfect strangers suggesting—*very* helpfully—all the ways you could do better than what you're doing.

Consider this a formal announcement: you and God, you'll do just fine. You were made for this. You do not have all of the answers, nor do you need to! Babies start small and simple so that our learning curve can grow with them. You are fully equipped to start with Him for every question a new parent might have. You are equipped because He gives you everything you need.

Contrary to the common opinions of others, there is no one right way to raise a child. Every child is as unique as each grain of sand. There are good practices, of course, and lots of paths to the same solution. Your journey will be yours alone. And if you have twenty more children, you'll learn that there are at least twenty ways for a child to grow strong and healthy.

In John 15:26, Jesus promised to send the Holy Spirit to help us by leading us in the truth. He helps us, step by step, to discover our values and desires as believers in Him. This helps us choose pathways for our babies. After all, He knows each child better than we ever will. He knows which will thrive on cold-turkey potty training versus a slow-and-steady approach. He knows who will rock homeschooling and who will be just the right fit for public school. And He has the very best for each family in mind, as well.

There's no need to be overwhelmed by the Information Age as you begin your parenting journey. Listen to your Helper, tune in or tune out according to His suggestions, and get ready for a blessed family life with Him.

☙ ☙ ☙ PRAYER

Holy Spirit, You are welcome to lead this family. Show us where to look, who to listen to, and how to bless each of our children along the way.

*I lavish unfailing love for a thousand
generations on those who love Me
and obey My commands.*
EXODUS 20:6 NLT

A little girl asks her mom to bring out her "doll box," a chest filled with over fifty dolls from around the world. Her mom had collected those dolls when she was young. Mom doesn't ever touch them now. But her daughter loves to take each doll out, unwrap it gently from its fragile tissue, and lay it on the rug. She repeats the process until there's a large pile of paper to one side, and vintage dolls spread all over the floor. Some have blinking eyes. Some wear the native clothing of Sicily, Japan, or Mongolia. The little girl doesn't know a thing about these countries. The dolls are not fancy or expensive. But she knows they're valuable to her mom, and she treasures each one.

The words we say to our children are like valuable little nuggets they can treasure. Each one is unique. It costs very little. Once you say something, you don't hold onto it—the kind word is there for the other to pick up and tuck somewhere special in their heart to unwrap over and over again, reminding themselves of the beautiful truth of who they are.

Others will say things throughout your child's life that will be worth remembering. But you as their parent can build up your child in the most important and unique ways. As a new parent, you might wonder if it's too early to start encouraging your baby. But, first of all, if you start now you'll be in the habit in a couple of years when your child will truly understand. And, secondly, write things down. Stick them someplace you can pull out later to give to your child. When they're old enough, you can show your child what good things you observed as they grew. Was he or she quick to laugh? A quiet observer? Full of boldness? Tender with an older or younger sibling? When they're older, your child will treasure the words you spoke over them from the youngest age.

 PRAYER

Dear God, help me to see my baby
the way You created him or her. Help me
take note of the things that make
my baby special so that my little one
will be able to treasure all the good words
I speak over my child.

YOU GOTTA LET GO

*The LORD is a compassionate
and gracious God, slow to anger and
abounding in faithful love.*

EXODUS 34:6 CSB

Socks and stale animal crackers pepper the floor of the car seat row. Dishes taunt you from the spot next to the sink that you always used to keep cleared. Bouncers, blankets, and stuffies clash with your sharp-looking living room decor—but they sure make your everyday life a little easier. Your home used to be fit for visitors, you think. But now it's fit for daycare.

It might take some time for your heart to adjust to the realities of parenthood. Fortunately, you have just that. *Time.* God is at work, making the heart look more like His every day. There's no rule book that says your home must sparkle before having people over. But we *are* called to practice hospitality. There's no Academy of Parenting recommendation that your car be vacuumed once a week. But we are called to have grace for everyone—especially our kids. There's no article in *Good Housekeeping* saying that unwashed dishes are a sign of a lazy spouse. But we *are* called to love, respect, honor, and cherish the one we've devoted our life

154

to. None of these things are life-changing or catastrophic. But as we discover very quickly, parenting brings about a whole new layer of exposure to the things in our heart. And little by little, we learn to let go of the less important things in order to love the most important with the heart of Jesus.

The only thing that really harms us is the way frustration, anger, discontent, and resentment fester in our heart if we let them. One of the best antidotes to the harmful thoughts and feelings is gratitude.

A year ago we were still wondering whether we could get pregnant, and now I have baby puke on my shirt. That's awesome!

All of these books are helping my baby develop a wonderful imagination! I can't wait to play make-believe with her when she's older.

I'm so thankful that we have a dishwasher I can load as soon as the baby goes down.

As God refines us, He helps us let go and focus on what's truly worth our energy. And that will make us the peaceful, loving parents He has designed us to be.

 PRAYER

*Lord, help me see the blessing
in every little mess. Amen.*

MY HELP COMES

FROM THE LORD,

WHO MADE

HEAVEN AND

EARTH!

PSALM 121:2 NLT

YOU'LL HAVE HARD DAYS

These trials will show that your faith is
genuine. It is being tested as fire tests and
purifies gold—though your faith is
far more precious than mere gold.
I PETER 1:7 NLT

Raising a child is an intensely beautiful thing. But as with all things beautiful, its intensity comes from the depth and complexity of taking the hard with the wonderful.

The seeds of a lodgepole pine are completely sealed with resin, which needs to be burned in order for the seed to be planted and take root. These trees are part of a group of *pyrophytics*, which means they need the heat of fire or the chemicals of smoke in order to reproduce.

If you were a lodgepole pine, you just might experience two different feelings when you got the first hint of smoke off in the distance. One: "Oh no, this will hurt!" And two: "Awesome, now I can pass my legacy on to the next generation!"

Friend, there will be times you'll wonder whether you were really cut out for parenthood after all. The baby will cry for an hour. The hormones will surge, you might drop an entire bottle of detergent on the floor while doing laundry, you and the spouse might have a tough disagreement—any number of things could send a day spiraling. Sometimes you can kick yourself out of a funk. And some days all you can do is wait for bedtime and hope for better dreams than the realities of the day. No one loves being refined or challenged. But when we have faith in Jesus, we know that the fire of refinement leads to a much sharper, more beautiful view of the world.

It's good to remember that hard days will come. It's even better to remember that hard days will go. After all, you've made it through as many days as you've been alive. If you can hang onto the knowledge that every challenge is a chance for refinement and you'll be passing on a legacy of faith and growth to your little one, then the hard days just might start bringing you a smile.

 PRAYER

God, the fire of refinement is painful,
but I know it brings beautiful results.
I will trust You in the process.
Help me to grow and to model
the joy of faith in You to my baby.

YOU MIGHT GRIEVE

Blessed are those who mourn,
for they shall be comforted.
MATTHEW 5:4 NKJV

So much emphasis is placed on preparing for a new baby that sometimes we lose sight of the fact that, for several years at least, we will be saying goodbye. Goodbye to quiet couple time. Goodbye to disposable income. Goodbye to life as you knew it. If you've been married for a long time, the adventure of a new baby may really shake things up for the two of you. And if you're relative newlyweds, you may struggle with the thought of not having much time as just the two of you.

Let this be your permission, if you need it: it's okay to mourn your losses ... even amid all you're gaining. It's perfectly normal to cry in the shower, to be sad for the vacations you'll put on hold, to miss the quiet nights of staying up too late with popcorn and movies. It's okay to wonder whether you'll ever get pedicures or massages again, to calculate how many diapers a baby needs in a year and be overwhelmed at where else that money could have gone. It's a lot to take in. And God's been there before. Millions and billions of times.

In fact, processing through the tough emotions is a good thing, when you do it with God. He is the Comforter. He is here to walk us through darker days. When we trust Him with our less-than-happy feelings, we get to experience the warmth of His arms around us and the tenderness of His heart. When we hold each other in our sadness, God can weave threads of connection and growth around us as a couple. It's not fun to experience the grief of what we're losing. But once we work through it in surrender to the Lord, we're free to look ahead at all we're gaining.

There's no need to be afraid of the feelings you feel, even if they seem inappropriate. The Lord is not afraid. He's close to the brokenhearted. And in His arms, you'll find His comfort.

PRAYER

Lord, help me prepare for all the ways I need to be the kind of parent my baby deserves. Thank You for being close as I work through what is going away for a season. Thank You for giving me so much to look forward to.

FEEL HOW YOU FEEL

Be still, and know that I am God;
I will be exalted.
PSALM 46:10 NIV

Sometimes having a baby becomes one great big daily checklist. Snuggle him? Check. Feed him? Check, check, check, check. Change him? Get dressed? Get a shower? Clean something (*anything*)? Tell your spouse "I love you"? Mostly checks.

It's so important to slow down—mentally, physically, and spiritually—to truly experience this gift of parenthood. When God reminded us in Psalm 46:10 to "Be still," that came with a second command: to *know*. The Hebrew word for *know* in this verse is *yadá*. One of the definitive words for *yadá* is "to feel." Be still, God says, and feel that I am God. Let it sink into your bones—this knowledge, this awareness that *I AM*.

No baby ever lost sleep over a dirty dish on the counter. But when her mama rocks her, holding her close enough to see the light from the bedroom window dazzling in her eyes and considering the bigness of God in this baby, this beauty—every child ever born benefitted from such an act. You can shift not only the course of your day but the course of your home by allowing your awareness to center on the Creator of every cell in your tiny one's body.

There will be times when you're sad. Be still and feel the sadness. Turn your thoughts toward the Creator of feelings and know that He's not offended. In times when you're ready to throw or shake something, cry out to God with the force of your anger. Then be still and listen for His gentle voice to soothe your hurt. In the moments when you are overjoyed, turn your glee in His direction and thank Him profusely. Then be still and soak in the light of that joy.

Nothing can prepare us for the investment of a baby. And nothing will get us through unscathed unless we slow everything down and remember God—when we need Him most and when we think we need Him least. Even as we go for a run or have a dance party, we can be still before God and enjoy this life He's given us ... one feeling at a time.

 PRAYER

Father, help me embrace the fullness of time with my baby. Help me remember to be still physically when I can, mentally often, and spiritually as a lifestyle. Amen.

TAKE CARE OF YOU

My yoke is easy and My burden is light.
MATTHEW 11:30 NKJV

The hardest thing for a new parent isn't figuring out which end is up on a newborn diaper. It's not handling the new little cries that happen at all hours. It is finding time to *take care*. Self-care is important, but it often feels low on the priority list when the baby's needs are so front and center. But Scripture reminds us of the value of choosing rest and care.

After God created the heavens and the earth, "He rested from all His work" (Genesis 2:2 NIV). The Hebrew word *shabath*, translated here as "rest," can mean something akin to stopping and celebrating. Even God, who never tires, chose to stop and rejoice in His surroundings. How much more would we benefit from pausing and considering how we're doing and the blessing we're living with our new family?

Jesus was a busy man too. In order to get self-care in, He had to get up early to find somewhere He could be alone and pray (Mark 1:35). He knew that His connection with His Father was *most* important. As a new parent, sleep and other factors may make it near impossible to even consider getting up early! But what *is* important is making Jesus a priority. Place a devotional book and night-light where you feed the baby or spend time focusing on Him while the baby sleeps. There is so much grace in heaven for new parents. It's not about quantity but the fact that spending quality time with Him is as important as breathing.

There's a practical side to self-care too. Some new parents find that showering before the day begins helps them feel more secure and focused. Others are simply thankful to put on non-maternity pants every once in a while! Find the practical things that make you feel a little more "put together," and try to make those important in your day.

Remember that a healthy mama or daddy is going to bless your baby too. The three of you are a team now—so make sure you get what you need in order to thrive.

 PRAYER

God, prioritizing myself is hard right now. Help me know what is truly important. Thank You for the grace for this new season and for every moment I get to find rest and self-care.

FOLLOW YOUR INSTINCTS

"For I know the plans I have for you,"
declares the LORD, "...plans to give you
hope and a future."
JEREMIAH 29:11 NIV

Have you ever tried a new hobby that you ended up being really good at? Archery, for example—a bull's-eye, or close to it, on your first visit to an archery range? Or what about a three-legged race, finding chords on a guitar, or making meatloaf? Chances are, you weren't worried about how you'd do on your first try. You were probably surprised and happy that you were able to accomplish something new with positive results. You may have been encouraged to try again and maybe even continued learning that craft or skill.

Parenting comes at higher stakes than tying your leg to someone else's and running a few yards without falling. But since we're made in God's image and He's the perfect Father, we most certainly have the instincts to be a great parent. You may experience happiness at the first small wins—soothing your baby's cry, successfully latching to feed, perfecting the swaddle—and feel encouraged that maybe you can do this thing. Bigger and more complex challenges will certainly come, but in the beginning, you and your baby will learn the most basic of life skills. And you'll quickly see that it's not as scary as it feels before birth.

Remember, billions and trillions of parents have gone before you. The amazing humans in your life now are the result of a thousand generations of parents loving their kids. In fact, you are too! And most importantly: God is there to lead, show grace, forgive, refine, and help, every step of the way.

The bottom line is, don't be afraid. Trust your gut. Trust in God. You and your baby will do just fine.

 PRAYER

God, thank You for giving me instincts that are in tune with You and with my baby's needs. Continue to refine those areas, teaching me to lean on You and act with confidence and grace.

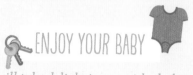

ENJOY YOUR BABY

He will take delight in you with gladness.
ZEPHANIAH 3:17 NLT

You have one main objective with your new baby: to enjoy. The details will work themselves out. Sure, you will have problems to solve. Every newborn comes with built-in surprises, whether or not they have a perfect APGAR score. But you and your spouse will figure out those things. It all comes with the territory.

But if you know those things up front—that there will be problems to solve and solutions to discover—you can relax and enjoy the ride. Because, really, having a baby is meant to be wonderful. It's meant to draw us back to a simpler lifestyle. It's meant to remind us that there really is something to that "faith like a child" phrase. Watch your little one and see how much trust they have in you from day one. Your baby is not afraid of falling; they know you will hold them. Your baby is not afraid of starving; they know you'll feed them when they ask. As soon as your baby is able, he or she will recognize your face and smile. Your baby doesn't know if you said something you shouldn't have yesterday or if your clothes are trendy today. Your little one doesn't care what kind of car you drive or how old you were when you learned to walk. Your baby instinctively, unconditionally, easily loves you. And that, friend, is how we are free to feel about our Father in heaven.

God enjoys us. He really does! And since we are made in His image, we are designed to enjoy our own children. So, please, give yourself permission to just spend time with your baby. Watch your child sleep or wiggle. Make eye contact. Make faces. Get super excited when they kick a toy or roll over. Make your little one feel like the most important little person in the world. It will do your heart good to treat your child the way God sees you. And it's true—before you know it, the time will have gone by. This is your one chance to revel in the beauty of new parenthood.

ℓ ℓ ℓ PRAYER

Father, thank You for loving me with
a Father's love. Teach me to slow down
and truly savor each moment with my baby,
just as You do with me.

YOUR TOUCH MATTERS

He will cover you with His feathers,
and under His wings you will find refuge.
PSALM 91:4 NIV

Did you know that skin time with mama (diapered baby on mama's bare chest) can regulate a newborn's own body temperature? If the baby is cold, mama can warm her. If the baby is too hot, mama can cool her, regardless of mama's own temperature. Skin time with daddy doesn't regulate in quite the same way, but it can warm a newborn to the proper temperature.

Your touch is how your little one learns the contours of their body. Your touch soothes, massages, and warms your baby. In the days before their eyesight becomes clear, your touch can be the centering point for your baby. It speaks volumes before words can be used to communicate. Your touch is the very best way to say "I'm here. I love you. You are my child and you're safe with me. Welcome to the world!"

Even when a baby is crying at the top of their lungs, your touch can make a difference. How you hold your child can help that air bubble work its way up or down. A sweet sway or light bounce can mimic their experience in the womb. It's impossible to spoil your little one in the early months by holding him or her too much. Letting your baby sleep on you or even baby-wearing throughout the day during regular activities simply serve to affirm your child's place close to your heart.

Even God, in all His greatness, holds us close with His touch. In Psalm 139:10 it is His right hand that keeps us close. In Psalm 91:4 we are tucked into His feathers. In Psalm 27:10 God assures us that His willingness to hold us in His arms is even more powerful than our own parents' love.

When all else fails, a sincere hug will speak volumes to your child. In the middle of the night, when bad dreams or fevers or teething interrupts sleep, your arms will be the comfort your child needs. Take courage in the fact that sometimes all your baby needs is to feel you physically close, while God does the rest. Your touch is a tool that will keep you and your baby connected.

PRAYER

God, thank You for letting me know
Your loving touch in my life. Help me to reflect
the comfort of Your touch to my baby.

YOU CAN'T MESS THIS UP

When you first have a baby, you seem to worry about everything. But you know what? Everything seems to work out. Everything—from fevers to diaper rashes or loving your child enough and hoping they love you—becomes an opportunity for worry. It's only through time and trust, experience and prayer, that we walk through it all, little by little, and learn.

If you are prone to worry, here are a few Scriptures that can help. Look them up, memorize them, or just take them to heart when you need them most.

When you lie down, you will not be afraid; when you lie down, your sleep will be sweet.
PROVERBS 3:24 NIV

Seek first the kingdom of God and His righteousness, and all these things shall be added to you.
MATTHEW 6:33 NKJV

For this child I prayed, and the LORD has granted me my petition.
I SAMUEL 1:27 NKJV

Look, I am making everything new!
REVELATION 21:5 NLT

Children are a gift from the LORD;
they are a reward from Him.
PSALM 127:3 NLT

I can do everything through Christ,
who gives me strength.
PHILIPPIANS 4:13 NLT

He will feed His flock like a shepherd;
He will gather the lambs with His arm ... and
gently lead those who are with young.
ISAIAH 40:11 NKJV

A quick Internet search will help you find so many more Scriptures leading to peace and fearlessness. Most importantly, always remember that God is with you. He is for you. He loves you more than you can imagine, sees you even when no one else does, and cares for you with His whole heart. The same can be said about your baby! So rest assured that no part of parenting has to be done alone. God has designed you for just this moment, this season, this life, this child, this family. You are His protégé. And your baby is His blessing. Stay close to Him and you'll parent like a pro in no time.

 PRAYER

Father, I give this baby to You
with my whole heart. I trust You to lead me
in parenting, for the benefit of my child
and for Your glory. Amen.

YOU WILL SHOW ME
THE PATH OF LIFE;
IN YOUR PRESENCE
IS FULLNESS OF JOY;
AT YOUR RIGHT HAND
ARE PLEASURES
FOREVERMORE.

PSALM 16:11 NKJV

LIVE YOUR FAITH

Dear Friend,

This book was prayerfully crafted with you, the reader, in mind. Every word, every sentence, every page was thoughtfully written, designed, and packaged to encourage you—right where you are this very moment. At DaySpring, our vision is to see every person experience the life-changing message of God's love. So, as we worked through rough drafts, design changes, edits, and details, we prayed for you to deeply experience His unfailing love, indescribable peace, and pure joy. It is our sincere hope that through these Truth-filled pages your heart will be blessed, knowing that God cares about you—your desires and disappointments, your challenges and dreams.

He knows. He cares. He loves you unconditionally.

BLESSINGS!
THE DAYSPRING BOOK TEAM

Additional copies of this book and other DaySpring titles can be purchased at fine retailers everywhere.
Order online at <u>dayspring.com</u>
or
by phone at 1-877-751-4347